GW00890402

Get That Gate!

Written by:

Leslie H. (Bob) Mead

Illustrated by:

Joanne M. Mead

2022

Leslie H. (Bob) Mead

ISBN: 0-9768550-0-3
        978-0-9768550-0-2

Printed and bound in the United States by: BookMasters, Inc.

Cover design by Joanne M. Mead

INTRODUCTION

Very seldom do I write a letter. Maybe one or two letters go to my daughter, Lynn and her husband Chris. She says my letters are interesting and funny. I told her they were not supposed to be funny, but she insisted they are and that I should write a book. Well, if a book is written, it will be because she insisted I put some of my stories on paper.

SPECIAL THANKS

Thanks to my wife, Joanne for doing the sketches and for helping me with my spelling.

Thank you, to Lynn Moncus for her time reading, correcting mistakes, and giving me some ideas.

Thanks to my daughter and son-in-law, Lynn and Chris, for doing the final corrections, putting my story on the computer, and ready for the publisher.

PREFACE

This book is intended to bring a little joy to each one who reads it, a smile to your lips, and even make you laugh right out loud at times. If it does this, then I have accomplished what I set out to do. I hope this book helps you relive a few memories of your own.

HOMESTEAD

My Dad's Folks settled in the eastern part of Kansas when they came to the United States from England. That is where he was born and raised. When a very young man, my Dad joined the U.S. Navy. The ship he was on traveled from San Francisco to the Philippines, Japan, and China. This was from 1906 to 1910. I don't know what he did for the next four or five years, but when World War One began, he was sent a greeting from the President to return to the Navy.

After this tour of duty, my dad, H.H. Mead, lived on a homestead on which he farmed and ranched near Norton, New Mexico, southeast of Tucumcari. My dad's sister and her husband, Will and Flora Kettle had also filed on a homestead there, and I think their property joined.

They also had some neighbors and friends named, Ford. After they left Norton, and moved to Denver, Will and Flora often wrote letters to my Mother, Lillie Mead, and asked about the Fords. The Abercrombie's were also some of my dad's neighbors. Mr. Abercrombie and my Dad played their fiddles and other stringed instruments at community gatherings.

The days, I imagine were long and lonesome, living about twenty miles from town, and neighbors being about one to two miles away. Transportation was either on foot, horseback, or by Model "T" Ford.

I came across this poem that my dad wrote about seventy-five years ago. It had never been published, and not read by many, so I'll put it here. It may be amusing to some of you.

Radio Friends

Sitting in my cabin home alone,
On the plains of New Mexico,
The day's work o'er and chores laid by
Until the rise of sun next day;
Hard pan biscuits, twisted out of dough,
Baked in oven crude by coals aglow,
Sweet memories bring back of long ago,
Now twilight of Old Mother dear, a pal of mine,
How I wish for her in radio time.

No friend goes, no friend comes,
None go, except animal life,
Never had a wife,
Luxuries none, until radio comes,
A little box, crude in itself.

From spirits dance, speak, enchant,
From W.O.S. I hear a rampant, mystery,
Sunday's grant of God, for rest,
His pulpit, choir, far away,
But in my cabin hear him say,
Sinners get ready for Judgment Day.
The choir, too, was here,
Right in my cabin home;
Spirit, "Holy City" song rang out,
And then a prayer, money too, dropped in a pan.
Sorry Rev I'm where I am,
But you know sir, the fireplace
And the glow is Church to me.

Service goes in waves to him who knows,
Conscience hears, the heart beats fast,
Memories first in life are last to fall,
Cause Mother loved us best of all.

So wonder mighty dream long,
If radio is not God's own wave song,

Tell it to the world, he says in Psalms,
We shall know and hear him in every chime,
So God's prayer comes to me in radio of mine.

By H. H. Mead

Maybe you can imagine a homesteader's cabin, without all of the modern conveniences we have today, nor any close neighbors. The community did have get-to-gathers such as dances at someone's home. Some of the time, people from around the community gathered at my Grandparent's home. They would also host church dinners as well as church parties. I think my Dad played his fiddle at some of these gatherings, and I guess that is where he met my Mother. Later they were married, turned the land back to the government or the bank and moved to Colorado to start all over and raise a family. About three years later, in 1929, I, Leslie Mead, was born.

BORN TOO SOON
OR TOO LATE

Of all times to be born, I picked about the worst. It happened only a month and a half before the big stock market crash in October 1929. Herbert Hoover was President of the United States, and as for my family and me, he was the main cause of the crash and all of the hardship and suffering we endured for years to come. When Hoover came into office, things were looking pretty good, and he said, "Ours is a land rich in resources . . . in no nation are the fruits of accomplishment more secure." I believe he truly thought nothing could go wrong. He signed a bill to raise tariffs on farm products. This was to help the farmer, but it went too far. Tariff was raised on non-farm products also, which damaged America's foreign trade and contributed to the Great Depression.

Because of the depression, my life was changed from the start, forever, and by more ways than I can count on my two hands. Maybe it was for the better and maybe it was for the worse. I will never know. Who knows, I might have been a rich man, if I hadn't been born too soon or too late.

My dad died when I was a year old, which may or may not have been because of lack of money or proper medical facilities. Mother, being a widow with two kids, had to leave us with grandpa and grandma while she worked in Tucumcari for wages or looked for work. Jobs were very hard to find. There was always someone else waiting to get a job, so everyone had to do his or her very best all the time.

We didn't go hungry and was happy to have the food we did have. We ate oatmeal for breakfast, which was good for us, while other folks ate cereal from fancy boxes. For supper, we ate a lot of mush, which was corn meal boiled in water. At noon we usually had a good hearty meal of meat potatoes, bread, and usually beans or carrots.

Most folk's were buying cars to drive, but we walked wherever we went. When I was 9 years old, old enough to get a job, I bought a used bicycle. I spent most of my spare time fixing a flat or a broken chain.

We did buy a 1932 Chevy Sedan in 1938. We had to crank the old car by hand, so most of the time it wouldn't start. One time when it did start, Aunt Edna was going to drive us someplace, although we had to get gas first. On the way through the gas station she ran over the gas pump . . . so that ended our ride. We soon sold the car to my Uncle Ed.

LOST OUT TO A 'SOONER'

Grandpa and Grandma McDaniel started their life together around Lawton, Oklahoma. Around the turn of the century, 1900, they headed west. Grandpa ran the race for land in the "Cherokee Strip". He lost out to a "Sooner" that had already staked the land Grandpa was trying to stake out. This race was held in 1889 on a strip of land designated as "No Man's Land".

Some folks may not have given much thought about the effort it took to make the race for land in Oklahoma Territory. Families had to decide they were ready to pack up and leave the home they had, leave loved ones, as well as many of their belongings, to travel hundreds of miles in a wagon pulled by a team of horses. They camped out each night along the trail through unknown places.

Other families rode a train, planning to buy a horse in order to make the run. When they reached the town where they were to leave the train, they still had to travel by horseback to the area where the race was to be run.

When they finally reached the race line, there were already hundreds and hundreds of people already in place, ready to run, and more people still coming. Lined up as far as one could see, were horses and people who stirred up dirt, everything gritty, dusty, and dirty, with a continuous wind that kept the dirt a swirling around.

Imagine if you will, folks meeting new friends from all parts of the country . . . Kansas, Missouri, Illinois, New York, and many other states. People were anxious to get the run started. Maybe it was a day or two to wait, then down to a few nerve-racking hours . . . a few minutes to wait. Everyone getting panicky . . . finally the shot is fired!! Off in a great cloud of dust, the riders race, leaving behind the rest of the family to wait several days, or even weeks before knowing whether or not their runner was lucky enough to find a piece of land suitable for the family needs. Was he lucky enough to get "staked out" and not run into a "sooner" who already had the land "staked"? The runner then had to make some sort of improvement on the land before riding back to the courthouse to file his claim. At last the family would be reunited! They would *hopefully* be back onto their new land to continue making required improvements before some "claim jumper" took it over.

GRANDPA AND GRANDMA

Grandma and Grandpa came to New Mexico around 1905, and settled around Endee. Later, they moved to the Plaza Largo Community, which is on the road to Norton, New Mexico. They bought some ranchland there and called it 'home'. They continued to buy land to add to the ranch from 1914 to 1930. Because of the long drought and the depression, they lost the ranch in the early 1930's. Then they moved to Tucumcari, New Mexico where Grandpa did many odd jobs such as selling meat, cutting and selling firewood, digging graves, building repair or maintenance, etc.

The old two-story ranch house still stands beside the road on the way to Norton. The ranch has changed own-

ership a few times and more land has been added to it for grazing cattle. A new house was built near the old one. They must have done a good job building the old frame house, as it seems to be pretty well intact.

They must not have had too many wild parties in the old house.

GRANDPA

Grandpa was a rather short, stocky, strong man with a square jaw. He was a Scotsman, and I suppose that is why he had many saving ways and ideas. I always thought it was because of the depression, and that we didn't have any money. This instance goes back to a time before the depression.

Grandpa had a few hired hands or cowhands that worked on the ranch. He had just fixed one cowhand up with an outfit of tack, which included a new set of bridle reins. One day this cowhand's horse came into the corral with no rider, and the new bridle reins were missing. Grandpa was pretty unhappy about the reins. They began searching the ranch for the cowhand. They found the cowhand hanging from a tree where he had hung himself.

All Grandpa said was, "So, that's what happened to my new bridle reins!"

Another little story the family laughed a lot about every time it was retold happened back in the 1920's.

"So that's what happened to my new bridle reins!"

When Grandpa still had the ranch, he planted grain, to feed the cattle. This was dry land farming and he had a hired hand that always "knew just what to do". When this cowhand was told to do a certain job, he would say, "I was fix'in to do that." This got to be a real joke and finally Grandpa thought of a way to trick him. One morning, he told the hired hand to go out to a certain field and plant a sack of salt. Of course he answered, "Oh, I was just fixin' to do that."

Years later, when I was about five years old, we were living with my Grandma and Grandpa, who were in their late sixties. During the hard times I had a red and white tricycle, which I had put many a mile on and finally broke the handlebars off. I couldn't ride it any more, and the only way to fix it was to have it brazed or welded. Grandpa and I took it down to the blacksmith shop to get it welded. The blacksmith charged Grandpa twenty-five cents for the welding job. All the way home Grandpa complained about the outrageous price, and that 'it was nothing but highway robbery'. I continued to put many a mile on that tricycle. I think I got Grandpa's twenty-five cents worth and *more* out of it!

Grandpa tried to teach me a few things, and if I had paid attention, maybe I wouldn't have had to learn them the hard way.

Once he was going to show me how to sharpen a handsaw, but at eight or nine years old, I wasn't too interested in knowing how to sharpen a handsaw. So rather than pay attention, I got a handful of little pebbles and flipped them into where he was running the file across the saw-teeth, just to torment him. The next thing I knew he was chasing me around the barnyard.

If he had ever caught me I probably would not have lived to tell about it. I had to stay hidden for a long time. Finally, I slipped in the house after suppertime in hopes he had forgotten about what I had done. I guess he did forget about it or else he figured I got some of my punishment having to stay hidden and missing my hot supper.

Grandpa would start out walking to town or someplace to go talk politics or farm prices, and of course I couldn't go. After he had walked a ways, I would slip up and very quietly, and walk behind him for a ways. He was always talking to himself, and I'd listen until I couldn't stand it any longer, then burst out laughing. He'd wheel around, cuss me saying, "Hellfire and damnation . . .", then chase me back towards the house . . . just far enough to get rid of me. I finally learned when to stop playing the 'little game' before he got too mad and would give me a sound whipping.

After Grandpa lost the ranch at Plaza Largo, we had to move to Tucumcari. We rented a house on the south side of town. I remember living there when I was about four years old.

We had a pen to keep a steer or two and a team of horses. One day, I rode horseback with Grandpa to a pasture east of town. Then we drove a steer back to the house. Grandpa butchered the steer and when it was aged, Grandpa quartered the meat and put it in a big icebox on the back of the wagon. I would ride with him in the wagon pulled by the team of horses as we drove around town selling pieces of the meat here and there. He also killed a hog from time to time. I remember sitting by the warm oven of the old wood range stove eating cracklin's fresh out of the oven.

My Uncle Tom and Aunt Violet lived across the pasture from us. It seemed like a half mile, but it probably wasn't that far. I used to walk over to their house to get some butter and milk about once or twice a week. They must have had a milk cow. I remember Aunt Violet was usually ironing, wearing a pair of overalls. The churn was sitting on the floor so I would help finish churning the butter, then take the milk and butter back across the pasture to our house.

Even though their house was maybe a half mile from ours, I guess she could hear me yelling over at our house when I was playing or telling Serena something, because I remember Aunt Violet telling Grandma, "That's the loudest mouthed kid I ever heard." I must have taken that to heart because I am pretty quiet now, except when I yell at someone to, "Get that gate!"

It was at that old house that I remember my first whipping. My sister, Serena, and I were rocking in the old high back rocking chair, and rocking pretty high. Grandma warned us not to turn the chair over, but we kept rocking harder and harder until we turned the chair over backwards and broke the high back in half. Sure enough, we got a good whipping, and we had it coming. Grandpa was able to repair it, but the rocking chair wasn't as comfortable as it had been.

Sometimes Grandpa would help us carry in the firewood, and help stack it. I remember him saying, "If you'll carry a bigger load, you won't have to make so many trips."

Once in a while someone would hire Grandpa to do some work for them, and usually I would get in on the work. I remember we cut two big trees down, not very far from home. The only tools we had to do the job with were an ax, two wedges, and a crosscut saw. After the trees were down, we began to split the wood. This was probably going to be our firewood for winter and wood for cooking. Just before dark, we got our two big steel wedges stuck in the trunk of the tree. It seemed impossible to pull the wedges out, so we left them there for the night. The next morning, when we went back to work on the trees, the wedges were *gone.* I can't remember what Grandpa said about it, but I know somebody had to have worked pretty hard to get them out during the night.

SHAVING

Twice a week, Grandpa would shave. This seemed to be quite a task, at least compared to the way men shave now. There isn't much to it and it doesn't take much time. Well, in the early 1900's, it took a little more effort.

First, Grandpa would set up his little round mirror that had it's own stand, either on the table or kitchen cabinet. Then he would get a chair and place it 'just right' in front of the mirror. Next, he would pour some very hot water into his shaving mug and use his shaving brush to work up a good lather. Then, Grandpa would remove his straight razor from it's case and began running it up and down on a razor strap, or what was left of it, until the razor had a very sharp edge. Next, he would cover his face for a while with a very hot wet washcloth. In a little while, he would remove the cloth and begin lathering his face with the lathered up soap and brush.

Finally, Grandpa was ready to start shaving . . . scrape, scrape, then sharpen the razor again, and scrape some more. It seemed to me, it was quite an art to shave with a straight edge razor.

GRANDPA'S TRIP

The year was about 1936. Grandpa and Uncle Zack had decided to take a trip to Oklahoma to see their brother. One day Grandpa spent the biggest part of the day packing a suitcase he called a 'grip'. The next morning, Uncle Zack drove up to the front of the house in a big black automobile, a Packard. Grandpa told all of us goodbye and out the door he went with his "grip". As they loaded up, they talked about the grand trip ahead of them, and off they drove.

In two or three hours, Grandpa came walking back into the house. He was not wearing a hat, his head was skinned, and his suitcase (grip) was smashed. All of us wanted to know what had happened. All grandpa said was, "Oh, that old fool don't know how to drive a car!"

They had turned over on a curve in the highway on Route 66.

All the other grandkids probably thought Grandpa was a fine old man, but they didn't have to live with him, and only visited him once in a while. Folks in town probably thought of him as a real gentleman, and many were his friends. I suppose he was, but to me he was a mean old man. I don't think a day went by but he would give me a whipping with a razor strap. He and Grandma wore out a razor strap on my sister and me and then started on another strap. Grandpa said I was going to end up in the reform school. I didn't think I was THAT bad. I often wonder what Grandpa would think about the way I did 'turn out'.

It seems to me, if kids were disciplined now a days the way I was, there would not be the need for so many prisons.

GRANDMA

Grandma was a tall, thin, German lady with red hair that hung down to the middle of her back if it was not in a braid or a bun. It was usually in a bun during the day, and braid at night. She used a hot curling iron to put some waves in it before going to church on Sundays.

Grandma would send me out to chop some firewood for the cook stove. One time she came out to help me, and said, "You aren't 'cutting' the wood, you're just 'breaking' it." Well, I never did know how to 'cut' firewood instead of 'breaking' it. I couldn't see that it made any difference as long as I got it into pieces short enough to go into the stove. It could be that the difference is whether the axe was sharp or not.

Grandma used to say, "You're the meanest kid I ever did see, and someday it will all come back to you, just wait and see." Well, I guess it has 'come back to me', and then some, in many different ways. Anyway I think I've been repaid for all my 'meanness'.

When I was a young kid, I used to like to make all kinds of faces, funny or not so funny and some just plain ugly. Mother used to tell me that I didn't need to make faces because I was already ugly enough.

It was during the early 1930's that the Lindburgh Kid was kidnapped and that was the big news on the radio. My sister and I were rather afraid at night, thinking we would be kidnapped too. But Mother assured us that if we were ever taken during the night, as soon as it got daylight and he saw what we looked like, he would turn us loose. I don't think she really thought we were that ugly, but I guess it made us feel better about it. Anyway, she said those people took kids from people with a lot of money so they would get a large amount of money to return the child. We didn't have any money so we didn't have to worry.

At that time we always walked to church, and the summer days got very hot. Grandma always wore a big black coat, and when we asked her how she could stand to wear the coat in the summer, she answered, "I learned this from the Indians . . . What will keep the cold out, will keep the heat out too."

I remember a couple of the songs that I heard Grandma sing. She sang, 'In the Garden', and 'Dixie'. The only song that I remember my mother singing was, 'Just Molly and Me and Baby Makes Three'. Once in a while, I heard Aunt Edna sing the song, 'Long Long Ago'. They sometimes sang as they did their daily work or would sing whenever they 'took a fancy to'.

PLAY TOYS AND THINGS

My sister, cousins, and I didn't have many toys to play with, especially store bought toys. We had to make whatever we could with whatever we found to make it from. I would nail a piece of metal bent into a half circle on the end of a stick about three feet long. This was used to push one of those iron rims that came off an old wagon wheel. I would push the rim just about as fast as I could run. This was a lot of fun, for a while. Well, anyway I got a lot of exercise out of it.

Another toy, or at least something to make noise with, I took half of an old wooden shingle that had blown off the roof, cut little notches all along on both sides of the shingle, bored a hole in one end, and tied a string in the hole about four or five feet long. I could sling this around in the air above my head and it would sound something like an airplane. This was fun until my arm got tired, and then it wasn't fun any more. I'll bet a person could mass produce those today, made out of plastic, and sell them in Wall Mart all across the nation!

There was usually an old car tire lying around some place that I could roll and run along behind, and every

once in a while jump on top of the tire and ride over the top. The bigger the tire, the better the thrill. This provided a lot of exercise but wasn't too dangerous.

Oh! I almost forgot about stilts. I just saw a pair today that were store bought, but I had to make mine out of two lengths of boards about two inches by two inches, and about six or seven feet long. Nail a block of wood on each board about two or three feet from the lower end; these were to stand on. Then nail a little leather strap from the block to the two by two to hold your foot on the block when you're walking. I made a pair that was so tall I had to get on the wood shed to stand on them. Boy, I was really walkin' tall then. It was a lot of fun until something

made me fall. It was a looong way down. I have now realized why I'm so healthy today; all the toys and games I made gave me lots of exercise!

We didn't have TV. A boy name Bernard told about seeing a TV in New York. He was in my class at school about 1937. He described the TV as a box with a picture in it.

We did have a radio, and when there wasn't too much static we could hear some music, or a continued story on it. Grandpa liked to hear the news. He would sit with his ear near the speaker, trying to get every word. Because the radio station was so far away, there was lots of static and a poor signal.

THE BOSS

My sister, Serena, was always a small sized girl. She never weighed over ninety-eight pounds. She was two years older than me, and she thought she needed to be the boss, always telling me what to do and what not to do. One day at school, I broke a kid's pencil in half. I THINK it was an accident, and anyway he had more than one pencil, but he said he would 'git' me after school, so I had *that* to worry about for the rest of the day. On the way home, there he came. There was no way of getting out of the fight, so we started wrestling around. I fell to the

ground with him on top of me. He had me down and was beating on me when along came my older sister, Serena. She said, "Bobby, get up from there and get on home."

Well, it really wasn't my *choice* whether I got up, *or* that I was fighting. I would have gotten up . . . if only I could. Well, about the only thing that was hurt was my pride.

CHRISTMAS GIFT

While in grade school, I think the third or fourth, Christmas was coming soon. Our class drew names a week or so earlier to see who was going to get who's gift. Just before Christmas vacation, we brought our gifts to school to exchange.

I had drawn the name of the girl that sat in front of me. I thought she *kinda* liked me, but acted as if she hated me.

I bought her a set of porcelain or china dolls that represented 'the famous Dianne Quintuplets', who were born in 1934. They were very well known because they were the only living quintuplets at the time.

She opened her present, turned around in her seat and said, "I don't play with dolls anymore." That didn't make me feel so good, because I thought the dolls would have pleased any girl in the class. I was too shy to say anything back to her though.

Anyway, I wonder if she still has those dolls . . . probably not. She most likely gave them away that very day. If she did still have them, they would be worth a lot of money now!

SUMMER VACATION

I spent a lot of summers at House, New Mexico with my Aunt Tina, Uncle Wes, and cousins Donald and Jim. This was a lot of fun, that is, if you like hard work and long hours, such as hoeing weeds, picking beans, gathering horses, irrigating, herding the cattle, milking the cow, feeding the chickens, gathering the eggs, getting the eggs cleaned and crated to take to town, slopping the hogs, feeding the other farm animals, carrying water from the well, chopping wood . . . I don't think there was an end to it. It just got dark and we went to bed.

I was always up at daylight every morning, so it got to be my job to gather the horses and bring them in so they could be harnessed and hitched to whatever plow they were going to pull that day. My uncle called me his 'Little Horse Wrangler'. At that time of the morning the grass was wet with dew. It was kind of nice running through the dew-wet grass barefooted. All the kids went barefooted in the summertime. I guess this was to save our shoes for Sunday.

When I got back with the horses, it was breakfast time, and my Aunt would be trying to get my cousin woke up and out of bed. She would say, "Come on Dongie, jump up, come on now Dongie Boy, time to get up." This would go on for sometime, and kind of 'get my goat'.

Later in the day, when my cousin and I had to go to the field to hoe weeds, the sun was beating down and the ground was hot. We had to keep moving as we hoed or burn our feet, or find the shade of a weed to stand in, or else dig the hot dirt away with our toes to the cool ground underneath and stand in that.

Each of us carried a jar of water wrapped in a piece of toe-sack (burlap or gunny sack) and soaked wet so the

BACK TO THE FIELDS.

water would stay cool a little longer. At the field, we put the jars of water in the shade of tumbleweed, so every time we made a round, that's to the end of the field and back, we could get a drink of water. Oh, for the good 'ole days! But that was just part of life as we knew it, we were used to hard work, and a good days work never hurt anyone.

My cousin and I hoed the weeds out of the cornfield and bean field day in and day out, except on Saturday and Sunday. After we got the eggs and cream ready, we were able to go to the town of House, New Mexico, to trade the eggs and cream for groceries, and we were each given a treat of a Baby Ruth candy bar. Boy, that was something to look forward to. After the eggs and cream were sold or traded for groceries, there were some items that were bought at one of the two hardware stores, and then it was time to head back home.

On Sundays we drove about ten miles over some real rough rutted roads to a community called Hassell for Sunday school and Church. We picked up a few kids along the way.

The people in Hassell called me, "Little black haired boy from House," because I had dark hair and dark complexion due to all the time I spent working and playing in the sun.

When the beans were ready to harvest, my Uncle hitched the team of horses to what he called a 'knife'. It was a rig kind of like a sled with a seat on it, and two long sharp blades coming out on each side at the bottom. He drove the team between the rows of beans, and the blades were supposed to cut two rows of beans on each side, that is, cut the bean plant just under the ground. All my Aunt, cousin, Serena, and I had to do was come along with pitchforks, gather the beans, and put them in piles every few feet.

There didn't seem much to that, and there wouldn't have been if all of the bean plants had gotten a good, clean cut.

It seemed the rows on my Aunt and cousin's side were cut right through. The blade must have not been adjusted right or maybe it was dull, anyway, Serena and my side was not getting a clean cut at all, so we would continuously have to reach down and pull the vine out of the ground instead of just picking them up with the pitchfork. We were getting farther and farther behind all the time. My Aunt and cousin were just laughing and talking and going right along with the greatest of ease piling beans, while Serena and I were almost ready to cry because we couldn't keep up, and it wasn't our fault.

Well, at the end of the week, I had had all of this I could take. My Uncle was going back to Tucumcari, so I packed my clothes and went with him. He let me out of his car in front of our house, and I went inside with my suitcase. My Grandpa, Grandma, and another Aunt who lived with us were sitting in the living room reading the newspaper, when I announced I was home. They must have thought, "Oh no, not him, back so soon, could summer be over already?" No one even looked up from his or her reading to greet me. I sure felt unwanted and unwelcome.

Well, the next time my uncle came back to town, I had my suitcase packed and ready to go home with him again, even if it meant piling more beans. Well, I was lucky and all the beans had been cut and piled by then.

Many other jobs needed to be done that summer, so my uncle found another one for me. We hitched the team of horses to a "go devil" similar to the same kind of outfits that he cut the beans with, only this one was to cut the weeds between the rows of corn. We went down to the field and he showed me how to drive the team so as not to cut the corn, but to get the weeds, turn around at the end of the field, get back in the next set of rows and come back. He turned the team over to me, and I *think* I didn't miss cutting *every* stalk of corn in the row. My uncle could see right away that he needed to find something else for me to do. I guess I just wasn't cut out to be a farmer.

TOO HOT

During one of the summers out at House when I was about nine or ten years old, my Uncle and Aunt took my cousin to Tucumcari, NM to have his tonsils taken out. Grandpa was able to come out to take care of things, such as milking; irrigating and keeping my other cousin Jim and me busy doing whatever needed to be done. One day Grandpa was irrigating the corn. Jim and I were supposed to watch the cattle, to make sure that they didn't get into the alfalfa or cornfield. There weren't any fences around the fields, so that wasn't an easy job. As the sun got higher and hotter, the ground became so hot it was burning our bare feet. There was a little shade on one side of the house, so we decided to stand in it for a while to cool our feet. That felt so good, we just couldn't go back out on the hot ground to herd the cows. Then I heard and saw Grandpa coming at a pretty fast pace. Jim didn't know to be afraid of Grandpa. Since I lived with him, I knew how mad he could get and that we would get a whippin' with the razor strap. I told Jim, "We had better run for it!"

There was a lane in front of the house where Uncle Wes had put the horses and strung up a barbwire fence to keep them in. When we 'ran for it', we ran out the front yard gate, and turned toward the fields. Jim had forgotten about the wire, so it caught him right in the neck and ripped a big gash in his throat. He was bleeding like a stuck hog.

I got him to the house where Serena and Clyda, a relative, were doing the ironing. They poured the gash full of black pepper, to stop the bleeding and someone ran half a mile to get help from a neighbor with a car.

The neighbor took Jim to the hospital in Tucumcari to meet his Mom and Dad. The doctor said that the wire came very close to cutting the main artery, and he could have bled to death.

Donald had a hard time with his tonsil operation. He was in real serious condition for quite a while.

This was not a very funny story at the time, but many years have passed and now we can joke about it.

DEBT

I started working at odd jobs for wages when I was eight years old. I knew where each dime came from, always kept records of how much I saved, and where I spent my money. I started a savings account at the First National Bank and made regular trips to put earned money in my bank account. I had a job delivering newspapers on a paper route when I was about eight years old. I also worked at Fur's Food Store when I was eleven years old. The account grew gradually until 1945 when I moved to House, NM.

I took money out of my savings account to buy a car. I have been in debt ever since. It's one car deal after another, car expenses, repairs, and fuel.

I had a friend named Marvin who I was only able to see on Sundays. He would either come to my house for dinner or I would go to his. Marvin always had a new joke or trick of some sort. Most of his jokes were original.

One day he said, "Bobby is just like both a Jew and a Negro. The Jew always has a dime, and the Negro is always glad to get one."

I guess he was right. I could and did save money at that time of my life.

MY COUSIN'S HOUSE

Once in a while, during the school year, when I was growing up, I would be able to go home with Uncle Ed, Aunt Ona, and my five cousins. They lived about twelve miles out of town on the road to Norton, New Mexico.

Their house wasn't very big; I think it had two bedrooms. All the kids slept in one of the bedrooms. If you have heard the song, "Sleepin' at the Foot of the Bed", by Little Jimmie Dickens, you'll know what I'm talkin' about. Four, five, or even six of us had to sleep in the same bed. After we had giggled a while, we told ghost stories until it was late. The rest of the night was spent pulling and tugging the covers on the bed. There wasn't very much sleep and it was misery until four o'clock the next morning the wind-up alarm clock would sound off and Uncle Ed would turn the radio on. We often heard Ernest Tubbs singing, "Walkin' the Floor Over You". Everyone had to get up, dressed, and be ready to start milking the cows. I don't remember how many milk cows there were, but that was an everyday, twice a day, event.

That was a weekend stay at my cousin's house. We did play a little during the day, usually riding bicycles.

ELBOW GREASE

While staying with Aunt Tina and Uncle Wes, at House, probably in 1937, we were trying to build some sort of plow or repair one. We had to drill a hole in the thick iron with a brace and bit, the only way to do it in those days.

It was my turn to operate the brace and bit, so I was turning the brace but the bit wasn't cutting into the iron to make the hole. My uncle said, "You'll have to use a little El Bow Grease." I'm not sure I knew what that was, but I did eventually find out.

My uncle said that he figured he could do anything he set his mind to. I think he was right about that, although it took me several years to figure out that I could do the same.

I've also learned to do several different things in my time such as make a fiddle and learn to play it, make and carve southwest furniture, draw, paint, build and add onto our house, raise and show Angus Cattle, and a number of other things.

SWIMMIN' IN THE HOLE

Sometimes during the summer, there would come a flash rainstorm to the Northwest of House, NM. Sometimes the rain would fill the draws with water and the water would come flooding down. We could hear the water coming long before the headwater got near. The water brought with it everything in its path . . . junk people had thrown away, fence posts, cow and horse manure, frogs, and more. When the flood was over, swimming holes were left, but they were not very deep. We could usually stand up and our head would be out of the water, so I never learned to swim very well.

When my cousin Donald and I were about fifteen years old we went to a church brotherhood convention where there was a large lake nearby. Soon after we arrived, my cousin and I headed for the lake. I guess my cousin knew how to swim, but I didn't. I had never been around enough water to learn how.

Anyway, we stripped off our clothes and went in. Right away I stepped off in a deep hole and went under. When I came up I gasped for air and yelled, "Help!" went down again, came up, gasped for air, yelled, "Help!" then went down again. When I came up the third time, my cousin was sitting on a rock nearby, trying to reach out to me. I gasped for air again and was able to barely grab his hand as he pulled me out. That ended our swim for the day.

I'm not sure I ever thanked Donald for saving my life.

DUST BOWL DAYS

Not too many folks are around today that remember the big, dark, dust storms of the 30's that came rolling in from the north. We could see a storm coming for a long time before it actually got to us, but when it did get there it was just like *nighttime.* We had to turn on the lights in the middle of the day, and cover everything with a cloth or some other cover to keep the dust off.

It was the custom back then to leave a few items of food such as jelly or jam, sugar and such things sitting in the middle of the dining table, so of course they had to be covered with a cloth. The dust filtered into the house and there was no way to keep it out. A wet sheet had to be put over the babies in their crib or baby bed.

One time we had been someplace in the old 32 Chevy, maybe out to Uncle Ed and Aunt Ona's house at Norton. On the way home one of those dust storms hit and we could not see *anything.* I don't know how we made it home, and I'm glad it wasn't my problem, but somehow we did make it home.

If you haven't been in a dust storm, it's hard to imagine just how bad they were. The dirt was coming all the way from the western Kansas and Oklahoma farmland that hadn't had any rain in a long time.

HANDOUTS

Passenger and freight trains came through town on a regular basis. During the depression of the '30's, "hobos" would ride any type of train they could sneak onto. Some of those "hobos" would jump off, or get off when the train came through town, I suppose because they were hungry. Pretty often, I remember when I was about six or seven years old, a "hobo" would come to our back door. I don't remember one ever coming to the front door. They would ask Grandma for a hand out, and she always gave them a piece of butter and bread or sandwich, even though our family didn't have much to eat ourselves.

I have heard that "hobos" left messages or codes for their friends or maybe just anyone else. They must have left a code about our house, because we got more than our share coming to the door for a handout.

There was an old colored man I remember most of all. His shoes were about a size fourteen, flat as a pancake, and black. He kind of shuffled the giant shoes along on the ground in order to get around. They were probably some shoes he had found someplace or were given to him as a handout.

ICE CREAM SUPPERS

Each day or so, something or someone reminds me of an occasion that happened many years ago. Tonight we had an ice cream supper. It reminded me of the ice cream suppers we used to have out at House, New Mexico once-in-a-while. Neighbors from all around the community would gather in at one of the farm family's place. Each family would bring a cake and some ice cream makings including rich cream, eggs, sugar, flavoring, and peaches or strawberries. The sun was usually just going down or had already gone down, because everyone had to finish their day's work, and then do the daily chores. Anyway, it was too hot any earlier in the day.

Someone had to go to town and buy a big chunk of ice, about fifty or a hundred pounds, wrapped in a quilt to keep it from melting. We would chip off some small pieces, with an ice pick, put them in a toe-sack and crush those pieces of ice with an ax turned side ways. These little pieces were put in the freezer all around the container filled with good ice cream ingredients, which was placed right in the middle of the freezer. Then we would pour rock salt in on the ice, add more ice and more salt until the freezer was full. The salt was to make the ice melt and get the middle container cold faster. Then the top of the freezer was covered with a folded up toe-sack or an old quilt or both. All the kids took turns sitting on the freezer to hold it down while some of the stronger folks turned the handle. Before the ice cream was made, everyone had a turn at the crank. It seemed like the ice cream would NEVER be finished.

Finally, the crank would get *really* hard to turn, and then it could hardly be turned at all. Then we knew the ice cream was ready to start eatin'. By that time it was dark and a little cooler. When we had eaten two or three bowls full, we were so cold we couldn't keep from shivering so bad our teeth rattled.

One time a neighbor kid said, "I've ate so much ice cream it tastes like Black Draught." . . . Now, if you didn't grow up in the thirty's you may not have heard of 'Black Draught'. It was BAD. It was a purgative medicine intended to empty the bowels, and it did. It tasted awful!

I ate a lot of ice cream, but it never got to tasting that bad!

A GOOD FRIEND

Every boy needs a dog to be his friend when he is growing up. I wanted a dog so bad that I kept pestering Mother about getting one for me. She told me she would do what she could.

Finally, one day Mother came home from work with a little blond pup. I named him Tony. I don't remember where I got that name. We became good friends, and he began to grow, and he grew, and grew. As Tony was getting bigger, we found out he was a German shepherd. I learned how to whistle really loud, so when he was out of sight, I would let out a loud whistle. In a short time Tony would come to sit at my side. Tony grew to be a big dog. I guess he might have been a nuisance in the community,

possibly going house to house for scraps, but I didn't know it if he was.

One night there was a light, wet snow. The next morning I whistled, but Tony didn't come. Finally, I noticed some tracks in the wet ground. They were the tracks of a dog being pulled with a rope, and he did *not* want to go. The tracks showed the dog was trying to hold back with a lot of strength because the tracks were deep in the muddy ground.

Anyway, Tony was gone and someone had stolen him, or someone in the family had had someone take him away. I never did know, but I missed him a lot, and didn't think I'd ever see him again.

After about two months, I went outside and there sat Tony, by the door! We were sure glad to see each other. If Tony could have talked, he might have had a real long story to tell about how he was forced to leave, where he had been, and how he got back home. I'll bet it would have been a pretty good story!

SMOKING IN THE BOX

The old ice box that Grandpa used to haul the meat around in the wagon was lying behind the house not being used. A neighbor kid came over to our house with a pack of Lucky Strike cigarettes and some matches. We went into the old icebox and lit up a cigarette each. It would have been bad enough if we had been out in the open, but we had the door shut on the icebox. Very soon everything was turning in circles. I was so dizzy I could hardly crawl out of the icebox and make it to the house. I just fell across the bed and lay there. The family called me to supper, but I told them I was sick and didn't want any. They wanted to know what was the matter with me. I told them I didn't know. Each member of the family came in to see about me. I'm sure I reeked with tobacco smoke, so they surely knew what had made me sick and figured it was a good lesson.

It was a good lesson. I never did learn to smoke and like it. I didn't try smoking again for several years.

SCARED HALF TO DEATH

While living on Third Street in Tucumcari with my Grandparents, James W. and Nellie McDaniel, my Grandpa got real sick one morning. He began walking the floor, moaning and groaning. I was only about ten years old and didn't know what to do to help him. Finally, the pain got to be more than he could stand, and he told me to run to town and tell Violet's doctor to come to the house *now* because he was dying.

Violet was my red headed aunt, the wife of Grandpa's son, Tom. Aunt Violet was the doctor's nurse. When Grandpa said he was dying, it scared me half to death, so I went flying on foot, breaking all track records, I'm sure. I ran to town, to the doctor's office, and up a long flight of stairs above the telegraph office. There I found Aunt Violet. I was almost to cry and out of breath. I told her Grandpa was dying and he wanted the doctor to come right away. She sort of half grinned and said, "Your Grandpa isn't dying." I guess she was already acquainted with his ailment. "Go back home and tell him to take an enema." I wasn't very pleased with what she told me, but reluctantly ran back home. Grandpa was already in the process of doing just what Aunt Violet had ordered. Soon he was feeling better. I was sure glad, because I was sure scared.

WE AND OURS

In 1940 or 1941 I got a job in Erskine's dry goods-shoes-and ready-to-wear store. First I was the janitor, and then I worked as clerk when school was out.

There was an old busy-body woman that worked there who I called, 'Old Lady Sparks'. She thought she owned the store or at least she acted that way. When she was talking to a customer, she would continuously say, "I don't have this." or "I don't have that." or "I do have that." Instead of "We" don't have this or "We" don't have that, or "We" can order it for you. This really got my "goat", but I never did tell her what I thought.

In my opinion it's the same way when you are married. It may have been "I" this and "I" that before, but after marriage, it should become "We" and "Ours". Isn't that what the marriage vows are all about?

WRONG NAME

Mother was a rather small person, not short, but almost skinny. She was never known to overeat, in fact, she didn't eat much at all. She was nice looking and didn't show her age.

Even though Mother was raised on a farm and ranch, she probably spent most of her younger days in the house helping her Mother, along with her two other sisters, instead of working in the field with the men. She probably didn't pay too much attention to the terminology of farming or the names of all the pieces of farm machinery. She then left home when she was married, and spent the next few years starting a family.

My dad died of appendicitis when I was a year old. The depression was going strong at the time, so my mother had to go to work as a waitress for several years and then as a cashier for several more years before she met and married a farmer from House, New Mexico in 1945. Here again, she prepared the meals and did the house work, not paying much attention to the names of the farm machinery but picked up a few names here and there in conversation.

We had been farming potatoes, sugar cane, alfalfa, and dry land wheat. We used a "one way' to plow with, a piece of machinery with a lot of discs on it that threw all the dirt in one direction.

Later, George, my mother's new husband, went down to another field with the tractor to plow some rows for planting and to be able to run irrigation water down the rows. He had a plow on the tractor with three plow points for the second job. Mother happened to see George as he drove the tractor down to the field.

A while later a neighbor stopped by to talk to George. The neighbor came to the door and asked where George was. Mother said, "He is down in the south field running a 'three way'. The man sort of smiled, looked down, and said, "Thank you ma'am." He went down to the field and told George what Mother had told him. They both had a big laugh.

There wasn't such thing as a 'three way'.

NORTHERN

March 'came in like a lion' in 1948. I was going to graduate (my fingers crossed) in May. Mother and George were going to have a baby any time. Just in case the weather did get bad, George had taken Mother to Tucumcari to stay with my older sister and be close to the hospital until time for delivery.

On the morning of March the 4th, we were listening to the radio, and a program at that time called, "This, That, Another, and a Guy Named Joe." We heard the radio announcer say, "We want to let George Griggs out at House, know that he has a fine baby boy, born last night."

It had come a real blizzard from the North that night. A 'Northern' we would say. There were snowdrifts three feet deep. We did the chores—-milked the cows, fed the hogs, fed the chickens and gathered the eggs, separated the milk, poured the cream in a cream can, ate a breakfast of Post Toasties, and got ready to go to town.

Then we went out and filled the pickup radiator with water from the tank at the windmill. We had to drain the radiator each night so it wouldn't freeze. Then we put the tire chains on so we could bust through the snowdrifts for about a mile and a half, until we could get to the highway. The road wasn't too bad from there on into Tucumcari.

Mother and Cary George, my baby brother were healthy and doing fine.

ARMY TIME

After finishing high school in 1948, I thought I had had enough of farming and ranching, so I went to town to find a job. In about two and a half months, I decided I didn't like that very much, so I joined the Army.

I was put in the Infantry and sent to Killeen, Texas or rather Camp Hood. That is just about in the middle of the state where it is *the hottest.* We crawled around in the grass and weeds among the snakes and lizards with our M-1 rifles, on our stomach and elbows, under barbed wire and other contraptions, practicing war techniques.

This went on for one looong year. We received lots of vaccinations, marched a lot, went on long marches with our heavy backpacks, stood in line for everything we did, listened to lectures, and learned to hit a target with several different kinds of rifles. The time went by very slowly. It was peacetime, so there wasn't any chance of having to go fight.

Every so often we had to put on our dress uniforms and march to the parade field for an inspection of some sort because some big General was coming, and we had to look our best. We had to stand at attention for a long time in the hot sun, so several of the GIs would pass out and have to be carried way.

On one of those days, we had gotten up early, went to the mess hall for breakfast did an hour of calisthenics, then back to the barracks to get dressed for inspection and parade. I had already drunk all the water from my canteen and I needed to fill it again before having to 'fall out'. The line was long with guys filling their canteens when the whistle blew and I didn't get any water. The whole Battalion was standing in ranks on the company street right behind the mess hall.

I had met a guy on the train on the way to Camp Hood. His name was Lowe, and he was on K.P. duty that day. As usual it was "hurry up, and wait". We were standing at parade rest, in ranks, waiting, and I was already getting thirsty. My friend Lowe happened to come out the back door of the mess hall to put something in the garbage, and a stupid thought flashed through my mind. I grabbed my canteen out of it's pouch, and yelled as loud as I could, "Lowe, get me some water!" as I threw the canteen as hard as I could. It didn't even make it across the paved street, when it fell, it rolled, clang, clang, clang, . . . very loudly. The company Commander yelled, "Who threw that canteen!?" The word quickly went all the way down the line to the Battalion Commander. In the meantime I almost wet my pants with fear! There wasn't anything to do but raise my hand and say, "I did it, Sir." The Company Commander said, "Report to me in my office after the ceremony today." So for the rest of the day, I worried about what was going to happen to me while we performed for some top officials. I could *imagine* all kinds of punishment. That evening, I somehow found the courage to report to the Commander's office, and say, "Private Mead reporting as ordered, Sir." He shuffled a few papers around, and then said, "What did I want to see you about?" I said, "I'm the one that threw the canteen, Sir." He said, "Oh, I see . . . well, see that it doesn't happen again." "Yes, Sir! Thank you, Sir." I had worried all day for nothing. I guess that was punishment enough, besides being so thirsty.

Finally the year I had signed up for was over. I had already decided that farm life wasn't so bad after all. I went back to House, NM and began doing different jobs on farms around the area.

I worked on a threshing crew, pulled broomcorn, helped build a big barn, did some irrigating, cut and bailed hay, and then got a job at the House Co-Op.

One year went by real fast, and then one day the mail deliveryman brought me a letter edged in red. It said, "Greetings. Report to active duty at such and such a place."

I was to be stationed at Ft. Sam Houston, assigned to an Army Medical Depot. (I had signed up for five years of reserve duty to get in the Army the first go round.) Now that I was trained as an Infantry Soldier, I was put in the Medical Depot to practice with a warehouse full of artificial medical supplies. The Korean War had broken out and that was the reason I had been called back into service. I thank God they put me in the medical depot instead of the Infantry, or I would most likely have gone right to the front lines in Korea.

We rocked along, practicing on the medical warehouse for some time, and didn't have to work very hard. We also didn't have to stand in very many strict inspections. That was until someone 'messed' on the floor of the First Sergeant's Quarters. The First Sergeant was not well liked by anyone. He was *very mad,* as you can imagine, and since no one would admit to the deed, we were all punished for quite some time.

Then it was time to go on 'maneuvers'. We loaded a train of flat cars with all of the Battalion's jeeps, trucks, artificial medical supplies, tents, and our personal gear. We rode passenger cars for several days until we arrived in Fort Bragg, North Carolina, or rather a wooded area someplace near there.

When we reached our destination, it was raining. We set up our tents in the rain, and ate our first meal out of mess kits, sitting in the rain. We lived in tents and ate out of our mess kits for about three months. Our Medical Depot was set up, and we practiced warehouse procedures until it was time to load up the train and head back to Fort Sam Houston.

There wasn't any room left for us at the camp when we returned, so we were sent to Camp Bullis, an old abandoned Army Camp about twenty miles west of Fort Sam Houston.

This time, we lived in little square huts or tents big enough for four cots and a stove in the middle for several months. Our duty was not very strict, except each one had to take his turn on guard duty, and walk the Post each night.

Another long year passed. I was finally returned to in-active duty, and able to go home!

BRAVERY

In 1951 I hired out to work on an unlocated construction crew. Our lineman crew was trying to dig pole holes in the malpai rock by hand and not gaining much. After several days of this, the foreman rented a jackhammer, so we could make holes in the rock for dynamite.

When we had all the holes ready, an old man named Mr. Head was hired to do the blasting. He had done lots of dynamite work in the uranium mines around there for years.

Mr. Head had an old worn out Chevy pickup that he carried his dynamite and stuff in. He would drive over to the next hole we were going to blast, tamp the dynamite into the hole, and attach the fuse to the dynamite. Then we would cover the hole with bedsprings and other stuff. Mr. Head would light the fuse with his battery while we ran several yards away.

With the fuse lit, Mr. Head would shut the hood of the pickup, get in, and "er, er, er, er, er, er, er, brumm", the old pickup would finally start. He drove away, just in time to not get blown up with the blast, and then on to the next hole to do it all over again. We watched as the bedsprings and all the other stuff flew about 30 feet straight up into the air.

TOO YOUNG
FOR LIPSTICK

While still working on the same construction crew, our crew moved to another little town kind off in the middle of the state of New Mexico. We were doing some work in an area that might be called 'across the tracks'.

This little story also involved some young kids. Everyone around the area came out to see what we were doing and watch us work. A Mother came out of one house to chop some wood so she would have an excuse for being outside. Her daughter, about twelve years old was peeking around the corner of the house, smiling. The little boy who was about seven years old came over to talk.

It didn't take the boy very long to get brave enough to ask us if we liked his sister. He said, "Do you like my 'seester'? She likes you . . . She wears the lipastick," and then covered his big grin with his hand.

Soon everyone was getting a little braver, and friendlier, and the mother would look up from her wood chopping long enough to flash us a smile now and then. The girl even came out from the corner of the house to show off a little. She was acting like she was mad at her brother for what he had said and chased him around, and all the while sending smiles our way.

Eventually, we finished our work there and moved on to another work area.

GOOD WATER

During the summer months, while working on the six-man line crew, most of the time several miles from town, drinking water was a priority with temperatures reaching around 100 degrees each day. We worked off this old WHITE line truck, which was Ma Bell green, and everything else was the same color. We had canvas water bags, like the ones that were used to carry water on the old cars crossing the desert on the way to California, and farmers used to take to the field with them. Anyway we had those hanging on the bumper, the mirror, and on hooks in back of the truck. Drinking from the canvas bags wasn't as sanitary as the individual water bottles they have now days. We made lots of trips to the water bags, with each one of us drinking out of any and all of them. That wasn't so bad except some of the guys chewed tobacco most of the day. So after one of them (I'm thinking if a guy named Curly) had a drink, the next person got a pretty good taste of the tobacco, enough to almost make him dizzy, if he didn't chew. Well, that was just part of the good life working on a line crew.

STANDIN' AND SINGIN'

Back in the early 1950's while working on the construction crew, a new young kid named Jim was hired. We were digging a lot of deep holes by hand. It wasn't long before we found out he could sing, so we asked him to sing for us. He sounded pretty good, and it seems his favorite song was, "Oh Fair New Mexico". He would stand, sing, and tap his heel and toe to the time of his song.

It wasn't very long before we realized that we were doing all of the digging while he was just standin, singing, and enjoying himself. We learned not to ask him to sing until the work was completed at the end of the day.

DAVID

While working on an "unlocated", or you might say roving telephone construction crew in the early 1950's, our crew was digging some telephone pole holes by hand. That's the way it was done in those days. We were building a line over to a little mining town a few miles east of the Arizona border. We had worked around one area for a short time when a little boy about four years old came out to watch us. As we got acquainted, which didn't take long, he began telling us stories while we worked.

One particular story has stayed with me all these years. I'll try to tell it the way he told us.

He said, "Let me tell you a story about a boy named David, I think, and then a big giant, and then there were two big armies about to fight each other, but one army was afraid because the other army had a big giant, and then they decided to let just one man fight from each side, but they couldn't find anyone brave enough, and then David was away watching the sheep, and then his father sent for him to take some food to his brothers that were in the army, and so then David came to where the armies were, and then David heard about the plan for one man to fight the giant. So, and then he asked if he could be the one to fight the giant because he had already killed a lion or two and a bear. And then they finally decided to let David fight the giant, and then they put a lot of armor on David, but it was real heavy and then he took the armor off and, and went down to the creek to meet the giant. And then David picked up five little stones, and then the big giant laughed at him, and then David put one little stone in his sling shot and then swung it around and around and let it go and the stone hit the giant in the forehead, and the giant fell to the ground, and then, and then, *They had one hell of a time!*"

58

FOOT PRINTS

During the crew's stay in Grants, NM in the middle of the winter, a friend and crew worker, Tom and I rented an old trailer house to live in. We thought we could save some money doing our own cooking, making our own lunches, and the rent was cheap. The trailer had an old oil-burning heater, that wouldn't stay lit. The nights were cold and miserable. There was about six inches of snow and when the clouds cleared away, so it turned even colder.

One morning after an almost sleepless night, tugging at the covers trying to get warm, Tom said there had been someone walking around our trailer during the night. He had heard the footsteps in the crusted snow crunch . . . crunch . . . crunch. He said, "I got up and looked around outside, but I didn't see anyone." The strange thing was, when we went outside there were not any footprints in the snow.

The next night, Tom shook me awake. He said, "I caught the guy slipping around our house." I said, "You did? . . . Who was it?" And Tom said, "It was *you,* grinding your teeth in your sleep."

Tom and I were not the best of housekeepers. The floor got dirty, the dishes were stacked high in the sink until we didn't have any dishes left to eat out of, and the rooms smelled of dirty clothes that needed to be washed. A dozen or so burned matches lay on the floor in front of the old oil stove that we tried to keep lit.

Once in a while our neighbor and landlord's wife, Rita, would come over to sweep and mop the floor. That sure gave us a lift at the end of a long, hard day at work.

Several farmers around Grants, NM raised large fields of carrots. In fact there were so many carrots raised around there, they had a carrot shed in which the carrots were washed, graded, packed, and shipped.

There wasn't much to do for entertainment around Grants, so some of us got an extra job working at the carrot shed. There were lots of cull (deformed and not sellable) carrots, so we could take a batch home each night. We ate so many carrots, in so many different ways; we were beginning to turn orange.

We ate carrot salad, cooked carrots, carrot pie, carrot cake, stew with carrots, and ate raw carrots. Carrot pie tastes a lot like pumpkin pie, and I do still like carrot cake.

CHUBBY

I went to a funeral today for my old friend, Chubby. We became friends when I was in high school in House, NM.

He had put in a little flat fixing shop in downtown House, NM. I painted a sign for him, saying, "Flats Fixed", only I stood the sign up too soon and the red paint ran down the front, so it didn't look so good. He thought it was great. We went to the same church, and I admired the way he always carried his Bible to Sunday school and Church.

I graduated from high school and then went on to the Army. It was there I learned to drink beer and dance, so when I came home from the Army, I guess I was a bad influence on Chubby and Pinky, my cousin. We would, after a long day of work, get a dollar's worth of gas and go pick Chubby up from his house. He always wanted to clean up and shave. He always seemed to leave a little shaving cream behind his ears that we would have to remind him of.

One Saturday night we went to Tucumcari to a big dance at the Armory. There were a lot of people there, and when we walked in, Chubby stopped, looked around, and said, "This looks just like the din of iniquity." I guess it did.

Some Sundays after church, I would invite Chubby and Pinky over to our house for dinner. Mother always cooked a nice Sunday dinner. After everyone had filled his or her plates, in a short time Chubby would say, "Pass the bread please, I didn't get but one piece to begin with." Then Mother would bring out the dessert, either pie or cake, and Chubby said, "When it comes time for dessert at our house, we just pass the *beans* again."

One time we went to the show in town, at the Princess Theater, and sat up in the balcony. The movie was a real sad one. The theater was quiet except for some sniffling here and there and tears in most everyone's eyes. Chubby pulled out his handkerchief, which was usually hanging halfway out. He put it to his nose and gave a *very loud* snort into the handkerchief. There were lots of laughs, and that sort of ended the sadness in the theater.

One night we parked some place on a paved road that wasn't being used very much. I think I must have been home on furlough from the Army, and thought I was pretty sharp at marching. I decided to demonstrate how to march.

I began, "Hut two, three, four, hut, two, three, four to the rear, march! Hut two, three, four, hut, two, three, four. They laughed and laughed. The more they laughed the more I marched. I'll bet that was some sight!

Chubby told the story of how he had wanted to go with this certain girl for the longest time, then finally got a date with her. After a while she asked if he had noticed her new dress, and Chubby said, "I thought I smelled new manure . . . I mean material!" I don't know if the date ended well, nor if he got another date or not.

Another little party was held along the banks of the big canal that ran through the town of Tucumcari, NM. It was full of water, but I don't think we knew we weren't supposed to swim in it. There were several of us, including a friend named Fred. He decided to jump in and swim. Well, there was a pretty swift current in the water that wasn't noticeable. Fred got scared and started hollering, "Help, help!" Pinky jumped into the canal, got hold of him, and we pulled them out onto the bank. Fred started crying, and said, "I'm a chicken s—t, I'm a chicken s—t." Pinky tried to console him, tellin' him anyone would have been scared and call for help.

One Saturday night about six of us boys loaded up in one car and started toward Fort Sumner, NM, just to be going someplace. Things were kind of dull around the small town of House. We stopped in Taiban, NM to watch the rooster fights for a while and buy some beer. Then we drove on to Fort Sumner and drove around town a while, and parked on the street to watch the people go by. We hadn't been there very long until the sheriff came up to the car and said, "You boys are not supposed to be drinking out here on the street." One of the boys in the front seat said, "We aren't drinking." The sheriff said, "Well, those boys in the back seat are drinking." To change the subject, one of the boys in the front seat said, "Do you know where we are from, Sheriff?" The sheriff said, "No, I don't believe I know you boys. Where are you from?" I think it was Chubby that asked him that, and his brother Cecil said, "We are from Ima." Chubby asked, "Do you know where Ima is?" The sheriff said, "No, I don't believe I know where that is." Cecil said, "That's where the hoot owls make love with the chickens in the broad daylight." The sheriff couldn't keep a straight face any longer, and had to laugh. Then he said, "You boys better behave and get on out of town." We went on back to House.

If you don't know where Ima is, it is northwest of House and Hassell. By Monday morning, word had already gotten back to House, about how rough a place Ima was. So you can't get away with anything in a little community like that!

Anyway, I hadn't thought about these things for about fifty years. I reminded my cousin, Pinky, about all those memories. He said, "I wasn't there."

BRONC RIDER

Somewhere along the way, I decided I could be a bareback bronc rider and compete in the rodeos. What gave me that idea, I can't remember. Going back to when I was a kid, my cousin Donald and I made a pair of spurs out of a piece of leather with a roofing nail through the back side to serve as the rowel, and tied in the front with a piece of binder twine. We each took our turn on a certain plow horse of my Uncle Wes. We had been given instructions not to try to ride this horse. We caught him and only put a bridle on him. Then my cousin rode him down to the field where we were to

change the setting on the irrigation water. He made it there all right and it was my turn to ride him back. We did o.k. until I jabbed my nail spurs into his side and he took off. I dug my heals in harder to stay on, and he ran faster. I hollered "whoa" but it didn't do any good.

My Aunt Tina and Uncle Wes came running out of the house just as the horse and I made the turn around the corner of the field and headed down towards the corral. The horse stopped when he reached the place where we kept the plows. I guess he thought it would be better to pull a plow. Anyway we didn't try that again.

We did try riding the yearling calves when no one was looking. We were not supposed to do that either. Somehow we caught them and held them long enough to get a rope around their middle, then one of us would get on, the other would let the calf go, and the rodeo was on. I was on one calf when it ran and bucked along a barbed wire fence where I cut my side and arm. If that was not bad enough, I was bucked off, or else I fell off, then the calf jumped up and down on top of me. I was hurting so bad; I went out

65

behind the barn and sat there. When it came to be milking time, I didn't help, as I was still trying to get over 'the hurt'.

Maybe I got the 'rodeo' idea from the guys I was working with years later, or the way we had to ride on the back of the Ford pickup over rough country from the Arizona line to Albuquerque, NM and from there to the Colorado border, north of Raton, NM. We were working on telephone lines, and had to climb the poles along the way. Our crew went over some mighty rough country, but riding a pickup and a bronc are two different things.

In 1952, I entered a rodeo at Ramah, New Mexico and came in fourth place in the bareback riding, so that gave me some confidence. Then I won first place at the Fence Lake Rodeo, and I thought I was really something. That night after the rodeo, there was an all night dance with lots of good fiddlin' music. I was feeling pretty good about my win. While out on the dance floor with my hat on, an old timer waltzed by and said, "We've all seen you . . . now you can take your hat off." Well, Ha! That sure took me down a notch or two, and of course I took my hat off. Since then, I haven't been seen out on the dance floor very many times with my hat on.

After two seasons of rodeos, and not another first place winning, the money wasn't coming in as fast as it was going out on entry fees and traveling, so my rodeo career came to an end.

Some of the other places my friends and I took part in Rodeos were the 'Cimarron 4th of July Rodeo' and the big Rodeo in Trinidad, Colorado, usually held the first of September.

I have tried to break some horses since then, even last year; I was thrown a couple of times. It hurts a lot more now and the hurt stays with me a lot longer, so I'd rather not ever be thrown again.

Two or three years ago, my youngest son, Regan wanted to do the branding the old time way by heeling the calves and dragging them to the fire. He had about three of his cowboy friends come with their horses to help with the branding. We used the horses to gather the cattle, and up to this time, my horse had done just fine. After branding, Regan wanted to mount up again so we could hold the cattle until the calves mothered-up. I hardly got in the saddle when my horse began bucking. It bucked about four big ones, and I was out of the saddle and had hit the ground on my chest. The fall knocked the wind out of me, but I was mostly worried about my two new artificial knees, which had been installed about four or five months earlier. The fall didn't hurt them and the other cowboys thought I had done a good job of riding, but I didn't think so. Regan said, "Dad, they put that horn on the saddle to grab a hold of."

At seventy-three years old, I guess it's time to hang it up. Well, no, we have a two-year old filly that is ready to be broke to ride. So . . . I better do that as soon as I can get around to it.

BAGGED WITH THE ORE

While working in the northern part of New Mexico, I decided to go over the line into Colorado. I had not been back to the state very often since my birth. Well, while over there, I met a girl named Joanne. We hit it off pretty good. After a date or two, she invited me home to meet her folks. Her mother was nice, and after a while, even her Dad and I were talking. Most of the boys in that area knew her Dad. He was known as a mean old man and not many boys came around very often.

Our crew moved off to Grants for a job there. You may know, Grants became known throughout the country because of its rich deposit of uranium ore in the nearby hills. Uranium was needed at that time to make atomic bombs for the war. The Government would pay big money to anyone who found uranium on his or her land in a rich enough vein deposit that it could be mined.

On my next visit to see Joanne, I talked with her Dad about the big uranium mines near where I was working. The landowners and miners were getting rich, the town was prospering, and everyone in general was making money. He got pretty excited, and began wondering if there might not be uranium ore on his land.

The next time I visited, I brought a little sack with two or three little chunks of uranium to show Joanne's Dad. He was thrilled to receive it, and that was about all the conversation consisted of from then on about uranium.

Joanne's Dad had been a rancher and cowboy all of his life, always had some horses on the place, and loved to talk 'horses' any time of the day or night. Well, Henry, Joanne's Dad had another daughter, Georgia that was going with a fellow named Ira. Ira was a cow foreman of a big ranch. Ira was trying to get on the 'good side' of Henry so he could ask to marry Georgia. Ira talked about horses of every kind with Henry every chance he got, but he didn't seem to be making headway. Ira, the cow foreman, heard about me seeing Joanne, and about the uranium I had brought to Henry. He told Daisy, Joanne's Mother, "I've been talking *horse* to Henry for all these months until I'm blue in the face. I still haven't gotten to where I can ask to marry Georgia. Along comes Bob with a tobacco sack and a little uranium ore in it, right away, he wins all of Henry's attention, couldn't do anything wrong, and could even *marry* Joanne if he wanted to!

COFFEE CREAM

One weekend, I was visiting Joanne before we were married. The family invited me to eat what I recall to be Thanksgiving dinner with them. We had been seated at the table, coffee poured, ready to eat. Several of the family members were there, along with some of the in-laws. Daisy, Joanne's Mother, asked if anyone needed anything before she sat down. "Bob, can I get you anything?" I said, "Maybe some cream for my coffee." She said, "Oh, sure!" She left the room and was gone for the longest time. It was too far for her to have gone to town, so I'm pretty sure she went out to the corral and milked a little from the cow.

Whatever she did, it was too much trouble and I was so very embarrassed, that I quit putting cream in my coffee from that day on . . . that is, unless the coffee is so bad it has to be doctored up with something . . . and the cream is *on* the table.

By Joanie Caudle

WEDDING BELLS

The day Joanne and I were married came to mind. That was about fifty years ago. It seems, the best I can remember, that I had a week or two off work between Christmas and New Years, so I went to Trinidad, Colorado to spend the time with Joanne. From there we went to a big ranch in Northern New Mexico, to spend Christmas with two of her sisters and their husbands who lived and worked there on the ranch. I think that must have been the biggest and best Christmas I had seen, up to that time.

While we were there, we decided to get married, but Joanne was still in school, and marriage was against the rules. The school wouldn't let her graduate if they found out she was married. Therefore we had to find a town pretty far away, maybe in New Mexico, to get married in. So we decided on Taos, New Mexico. Joanne and I talked it over with one of her sisters, and she thought it was a great idea, but the other sister was against it.

We were at ranch 'headquarters', about forty-five miles from a highway in any direction. The night before we were going to Taos came a real deep, heavy snow. We started out toward the small town of Cimarron. The road was so drifted full of snow, it was better to drive out in the pasture part of the time. There, we had to drive over fallen trees and big rocks that were hidden in the snow. I don't know how we did this, except that it was real cold, and the snow was crusted enough that we just drove on top of it. If we had broken through the snow, we would have gotten so stuck, we would have been there for days. We finally made it through to the highway, and on to Cimarron.

From there on, the highway was snow packed and real slick. We had started out early in the morning, but a lot of time had passed due to the bad road conditions.

The courthouse in Taos, where a marriage license was to be purchased, closed at noon so we had to hurry. We went off the road a couple of times on slick curves but thankfully, didn't turn over. Getting back on the road took some doing but as they say, 'where there is a will, there is a way'! Just before we arrived in Taos, there were several real sharp curves at the end of the canyon. Trying to make one of these curves, the pickup went into a spin. Joanne grabbed the steering wheel, and I slung her completely out of her seat, trying to get the pickup headed down the right side of the road again.

When we finally got to Taos, the courthouse was closed. We happened to see the Police Chief and told him our story. He said he would get someone to open up the clerk's office. When they let us in, Joanne had to lie about her age because she wasn't eighteen yet. They gave us the license, but we had to pay double because of the extra trouble. That cost us an additional two dollars and twenty-five cents! We only had twenty-some dollars with us.

Next, we tried and tried to find a preacher of some sort, but there were none in Taos for one reason or another. Then we were told about an old retired Baptist Preacher that lived out on Ranchito Road. We called him and he said yes, he would marry us. The preacher tried to give us directions to his house, but decided that we wouldn't be able to find it. It was agreed that he would come to town and marry us there. We got a room, dressed up, and stood out like two sore thumbs. People don't dress up much in Taos. The preacher and his wife came, the owners of the Taos Inn 'stood up' with us in the lobby of the hotel, and the people in the bar watched through the door.

We paid for the room, gave the preacher a few dollars, ate at a café on Taos Plaza, watched a picture show, and had just enough money left to buy breakfast. That's probably one of the cheapest weddings on record.

When we got back to the ranch, one of Joanne's sisters asked, "Did you get married?" and the other sister said, "They sure as h— better be!"

MIXED HERD

Joanne and I had not been married very long when Joanne's folks wanted to sell us eighty acres of their ranch. We jumped at the chance to buy it, even though we couldn't afford it. I had already found out if I wait until I can afford something, I might never get it. I had bought three milk cows from Joanne's dad, Henry, and before I had them moved, they all had calves. I had a friend out in the House, New Mexico community that milked several cows, so I made a deal with him to pasture my cows for the milk he could sell from them. I had a Ford pickup with a flat bed and stock racks that I had made, so we loaded them all in this pickup. I was on my way from Trinidad, Colorado to House, New Mexico. On the way through town I dropped Joanne off at her High School Graduation. She has never forgiven me for hauling them old cows instead of going to her graduation.

I was working in Santa Rosa, New Mexico, so by the time I got there it was very late at night, so I parked the pickup with the cows in it behind the apartment I was staying in. I had to work all the next day, so I wasn't able to take the cows to House until that evening. I'll never know what kept them from breaking out of those stock racks, but they didn't. To say the least, they were hungry, thirsty, and ready to get out of that little old pickup!

The cattle stayed there for two years or so, and multiplied to the extent that I had to start paying rent for their pasture because all of them didn't give milk. We decided to take the herd back to Trinidad and put them on 'our own place'. We bought an old single axle trailer, and somehow got all those cows loaded up in the pickup with stock racks and the trailer. Now this looked like some poor old farmer's outfit, if you ever saw one! The weight of the cattle in the pickup and those in the trailer was so heavy on the hitch that it almost drug the ground. We made it to Trinidad and only had one flat, which was a miracle.

Things rocked along pretty good for a while, and we bought our first Registered Angus bull to start upgrading the herd. The next year was a bad one. It didn't rain and the pasture grass died out. Then we leased some more pasture up in the canyon going toward Weston, Colorado. The grass there didn't last long, so the only thing left for us to do was sell the cows. The cow market was not good because of the lack of rain and pasture grass. The three cows were Jersey, their calves were some kind of cross breed, and then those cows had been bred back to a Shorthorn bull. Their calves were pretty strange looking. We took them to the auction sale in Trinidad. When our herd came into the sale ring someone hollered, "What are they?" Well, that didn't help an already poor market. We sat quietly, didn't say anything, thinking if we did, it would only make matters worse. The cattle sold for eight to ten cents a pound. The market today would be about one dollar to a dollar-thirty for that same kind of animal.

Anyway we took our loss just like everyone else and went home. We didn't have any cattle to worry about for a while, and later we used that money to make a down payment on our place in Taos, New Mexico.

HORSE TRADEN'

Along in the early 1960's, my father-in-law, Henry, had a market for a few horses around Trinidad, Colorado. If I was able to buy some horses around Taos, he would come over and get them and we could make some money.

I found one horse over at Carson, a little settlement across the Rio Grande from Taos. The owner had tried to break him, but let him run away with the saddle on. The saddle had turned and skinned up the horse's legs and hurt his back. The horse's legs had healed up, but he still had a tender place on his back that they said would cause him to buck. I took him home, saddled him and rode him around. I guess I wasn't heavy enough to cause his back to hurt, so he didn't buck at all. There was a dude outfit at the East end of Taos, so I rode the horse about five miles down the Canyon to this dude outfit, thinking they might buy him or ride him a lot and get him real gentle. They did take the horse for a while, but I don't think they ever used him. I think it was a good thing, or someone might have gotten hurt.

I found another horse out at the Indian Reservation. He was a five year old and had not been broke, but would lead like a little dog, because he had been led to water at the Pueblo Creek most of his life. I put a saddle on him, but didn't get too far before he had thrown me real hard. I didn't try to ride him again until one day my folks came to see us and my younger brother said, "I want to see you ride that horse." I said that I needed to do that, so I got him saddled and got on. He broke right in two, turned every which way, and then he threw me on some real hard ground. He was still bucking when he went out of sight and on down to the creek.

I decided that I'd better sell him before I got killed. So I bought three other horses from someplace, called Henry and told him I had these horses and I wanted a certain amount of money for them. A ranching friend and Henry came over in a truck and took the horses to Trinidad.

Henry had the horses in the corral, when one of his son-in-laws saddled the one I had ridden to the dude outfit. He weighed about sixty pounds more than I did so he must have hurt the horse's back. That horse bucked all over the coral scattering hat, cigarettes, and all the things in his pockets, everywhere. Henry got rid of the horses to some other horse buyer.

I think I had added on a few more dollars than I gave for the horses, and Henry had added on a little more for his trouble. Anyway this was something for him to make some extra money on.

I asked Daisy if Henry had made any money selling those horses. She said there wasn't much to make when everyone wanted to make a few dollars . . . meanin' me.

That was the end of our horse-trading deal.

PUEBLO HORSE

One of my friends told me about a good, gentle horse for sale pretty cheap, so I went to see him. The horse was west of Taos, past Ranchitos and before Los Cordovas, both were neighboring villages of Taos. The price for the horse was $150.00, which included a saddle, saddle blanket, pad, and bridle. It didn't take long to say I would take him.

My friend, Freddie was feeling bad that he hadn't bought the horse, so I left the horse at his house for the rest of the day. He and his kids could ride him, and then I took the horse home, up the canyon. But the next day, the horse was gone! We didn't know where he could have gone. We continually looked for him up and down the canyon.

About two months later we still had not found him, but one day I saw an Indian riding a horse in town. I thought the horse looked familiar, then I saw the big Indian brand on his hip, so I was almost sure he was my horse. I began talking to the rider, and told him I thought he was riding my horse.

The Indian finally told me that he had raised the horse at the Pueblo, sold him to a Forest Ranger named Ed, and he had sold him to a retired preacher. That is whom I had bought the horse from.

When I took the horse home, I guess he knew the Pueblo was just over the mountain a few miles, and that was still home to him, so that is where he had gone.

This was a good mountain horse and had made several trips to Blue Lake when White Man could still go up there and spend a week each year in September. We can't go up there anymore since the Government gave the mountain land, which included Blue Lake to the Taos Pueblo Indians. The Pueblo Indians call Blue Lake, "sacred".

The Indian's name was Onofre. He didn't give me any trouble about the ownership of the horse and let me have him back right on the spot.

CAN'T MAKE ME!

When I was eighteen years old, My Mother and Step Dad, George had my little brother, Cary. When he was still a baby, I finished high school and then went on to the Army. After that, I realized I didn't want to work in town, so when I got out of the Army, I got a job away from home. After Joanne and I were married, I got a job in Taos, where we settled. My little brother had grown quite a lot while I wasn't around. Then he was old enough to come stay a few days at a time, in Taos.

Cary didn't like 'this or that' when it came to eating. No one was going to make him eat anything he didn't want to. WOW! What a difference ten or twelve years made in the way to raise a kid. The things he could get away with or without doing was very different from the way my sister and I had been raised!

At breakfast one morning, my little brother, Cary, decided he was not going to eat the yoke of his fried egg. I don't know how Joanne did it, but before it was all said and done, he had eaten the yoke of his egg.

Joanne and I were in Tucumcari when he was about four years old. One day we decided to climb Tucumcari Mountain. Cary wanted to come along. We drove as close to the mountain as we could get. We were going to hike from there, but that seemed too far for Cary, so he was *not* going to go. Joanne and I started out on the hike and left Cary sitting in the car. After we had gone about a quarter of a mile, we could hear him screaming, "Bobby, come get me!" I had to go back for him. This didn't make me any happier. This time he came along, although I think I had to carry him most of the way. We finally made it to the top. We have a picture of the mountaintop view of Tucumcari, NM somewhere around here to remember the event.

ANYTHING FOR A BROTHER

Several years later, when Cary and his finance, Linda was to be married, we made a *fast four-hour trip* to Tucumcari from Taos. I had gotten off work a little late, a few minutes after five o'clock, and had to be to the church by eight o'clock.

I drove through the mountain curves with the power steering 'out' on our car while the family held their breath in fear most of the way. We made the trip in two and a half hours, changed clothes, and maybe were a minute or two late when we arrived at the church. We made the trip all right and would not have missed the special occasion for anything, especially for a brother!

SAVING WAYS

For fifty years, Joanne has been reminding me of how little money we had to buy groceries with. She says I only allowed her five dollars a week. That may have been the case for a little while, but she says it was for two or three years.

Joanne just reminded me of the time I started to work and came across a deer someone had hit and killed with a car. I threw the deer in the pick-up, came back home in a hurry, backed up to the barn, tied a pulley and singletree onto the hind legs and hoisted the deer up to the rafters. I told Joanne to go ahead and gut the deer, and I'd be back to put it in the old cooler.

She did dress out the deer, but she was pregnant, and the smell made her sick. She never could eat any of the meat without getting sick all over again.

This was one of my saving ways. I just couldn't stand to see that meat go to waste.

A DIFFERENT WAY

Joanne and I started our Registered Angus Cattle operation in 1958, on a very small scale. It wasn't long though until we outgrew the pasture at our home place in Taos Canyon, so we had to rent pastures in different areas around Taos. When we ran out of grass in one pasture, we just moved the cattle to another rented pasture. This was done either by driving them or loading them in the pickup with stock racks and making several trips. That was usually better than driving them because of all the drive way entrances to people's houses that didn't have gates to close or cattle guards. There weren't enough of us to watch all the entrances so the cattle would run into every lane they could, to check out the pretty green lawns, and lush flower or vegetable gardens. We met a lot of the folks around the Taos area and even made new friends as we collected the cattle along the way.

One time, when Joanne's folks came to visit us, we needed to move the cattle, so her Dad, Henry, gave us a hand. Now, he has been a cowboy and rancher all his life. All the cattle work was done on a rather big scale with big corrals to gather the cattle in, big trucks to load them in, and the use of suitable loading chutes. Well, when Henry saw the way we moved cattle he couldn't believe his eyes. I just backed the pickup into a ditch, tossed a little hay in front of the truck bed, and opened the tailgate. Two cows and two calves jumped in. I slammed the tailgate shut, wired it good with some bailing wire and away we went to the other pasture, dumped them out and headed back for another load until all the cattle were all moved.

When we returned home, Henry couldn't wait to tell Joanne's mother, Daisy, about the moving job. He said,

"Daisy, you should have seen how these kids moved those cows. I've never seen anything like it in my life!"

We did a lot of things differently than most folks, but it was mostly for the lack of money to be able to do it a better way. Now we have a bigger pickup and a 20-foot long gooseneck trailer, but sometimes we still have to put up a temporary pen of some sort to load them from.

IT'S A SMALL WORLD

During one of our visits to Joanne's Folks in Trinidad, Colorado, an elderly couple came out from town to also visit Joanne's folks. They were introduced to me as Mr. and Mrs. McKinley. I told them that there were some McKinley kinfolk in my family, on my Grandpa McDaniel's side of the family. Mr. McKinley asked what my Grandpa's name was, and I told him it was James W. McDaniel.

Mr. McKinley laughed and said, "He is my cousin! We grew up together. We used to ride the prairies horseback, and run down wild horses. We would get the horses tired out and then jump from our horse over onto the wild horse. We rode them a ways, called 'em broke, then traded 'em to the Indians."

This was quite a coincidence. The McKinley's had been friends with Joanne's folks for several years, and would come out to visit and buy fresh eggs. Mr. McKinley sat, drummed his fingers on the arm of the chair and kind of half way whistled. Then he told another story.

Mrs. McKinley was in a quilt-making group with Daisy. She had a favorite saying that they all laughed about. She always had to say, "It won't work!" no matter what they were doing or working on.

SHORT CUT

Sometime in my early life I got the bad habit of taking unnecessary chances, maybe to save time or work. Too often some of those chances didn't save either time or work, but caused hardship, lost a lot more time and work on my part, and sometimes cost others as it involved their time and work as well.

On one occasion, before Joanne became my wife, we were out driving around and decided to go to the livestock sale. In order to get there, we had to cross the Purgatory River. There was a bridge but it was down the road about a mile, and where we were, a road crossed the river that could be used when the water wasn't too high. This was in the middle of the winter, when the river was frozen over, so I figured we could save a little time, drive across on the ice, and be there sooner. The river was only about seventy-five yards across. We made it fine until we reached the other side where the sun had been reflecting off the bank onto the ice and the ice was much thinner. As you might guess, as we started up the bank, the rear end of the pickup broke through the ice and 'there we were'. We walked some distance to a telephone to call Joanne's Dad to see if he would come help. Well, he had to go the long route, and cross the bridge to the other side so he could pull the front end of the truck.

All he said when he got there was, "Damned fool kids." Anyway, he hooked on with a chain and pulled us out.

LONG TERM INVESTMENT

When Joanne and I came to Taos, there was only one Real Estate Broker, whose name was Doughbelly Price. He must have made a lot of money selling land and houses because today there are hundreds of realtors. I don't know if all of them make a living from selling real estate or not, but they give that impression.

Anyway, Doughbelly called his office, 'The Clip Joint', and each week he would have a little article in the local Taos paper, called the 'El Crepusculo'. It told about some

Doughbelly

new property he had on the market. Doughbelly would describe the property and then state that it wasn't worth it, but that's what the seller wanted for it. That was his way to do free advertising.

We looked at four acres of land down on Ranchito Road, for which they were asking twenty-four hundred dollars. I thought the water table was too close to the ground surface for it to be good to build a house on and decided not to buy it. Doughbelly said, "Well, if you don't buy it, somebody else will," and sure enough they did. That's another one of those mistakes I made. That property in the same area now sells for around thirty thousand dollars or more for each acre.

One of his advertisements did catch my eye about a ranch in Southern Colorado. He took us up there to look at the land. It turned out to be a small ranch of mostly sagebrush, a little valley running down through the middle of the property, with about a hundred acres or so of grass in the valley. Water running through there came from a reservoir at the far end of the place. He drove us all around in his new Chevy car. There was no road except for a strip where a dozer had cleared a path for the fence lines. We got stuck when we crossed a bar ditch getting back on the road.

I felt real bad because we had put him and his car through this ordeal, so we bought the place.

The place wasn't much money and the payments were easy. Maybe it has increased in value or maybe it's still worth about the same, figuring the continued rise in the cost of living. We have never used the place, and it is still the same as it was then, waiting for some irrational buyer to come along and buy a "nice little ranch".

Doughbelly always dressed in a pair of Levi's, white shirt, with a little bow tie of sort, black or denim vest, black hat, and boots. Quite often, I drank coffee with him in a little café near the middle of town. He always carried this tobacco sack and rolled his own cigarettes.

Doughbelly's newspaper articles were filled with misspelled words, no capitals letters, or if so, they were in the wrong place, and not near enough commas or periods. The newspaper office printed Doughbelly Price's news stories just the way he wrote them.

I think Doughbelly came to Taos about the same time as Long John Dunn, who was a fugitive from Texas, and started a gambling place over at Elizabeth Town, or 'E' Town. Dunn got rich and came on over to Taos where he started a freight business which involved going across the Rio Grande River. That's where he built the John Dunn Bridge. It is still there, but not used very much anymore, since a new bridge now goes across the top of the 600-foot gorge.

When Doughbelly died, his coffin was carried through Taos on a wagon pulled by a team of horses. His boots, saddle and other gear were on his horse, tied to the wagon. Taos lost one of its most memorable and colorful characters.

I am writing this story during the middle of February. We don't know if it is going to rain or snow. This weather reminds me of the day we came to make the town of Taos our new home. What kind to town had we come to?!?

We drove up the little hill just south of the Plaza. The water was running down the street like a very muddy river, with high banks of snow on each side. The potholes were so deep, I was sure a tire would fall in one and we would not be able to drive back out, or that we would get stuck in the deep mud. The only reason we did not get stuck was because the ground underneath must have still been frozen and there may have been some sort of paving under the mud.

This reminds me of one of Doughbelly's articles in the newspaper, in which he talked about the Plaza, which was in the same kind of condition as the street, with all the potholes. Even though he used to drive a jeep, he said, "A body has to pull leather when driving around the Plaza!"

TURKEY IN THE ROUGH

After Joanne and I purchased a small place in Taos Canyon, in 1957, I met an old man named Cornet. He lived in an old run down adobe shack in Cordierra, which is on the outskirts of Taos. I stopped by his shack one day and on a shelf were about three antique coffee grinders. I asked if he would sell them. He said he might sell one of them, but one certain one, he used to grind his chicken feed, he would not sell. He said it ground the feed finer than the other grinders. So I asked him what he would take for one of the other grinders, and he said, "Oh . . . 'bout fifty cents." I bought the grinder.

Ole man Cornet did custom plowing for people all around the area, but the difference was that he still used a team of horses instead of a tractor. We thought a big garden would be nice to have on our new place, so I asked if he would come out and plow the ground. He was glad to get the job, and came out to the place early the next day.

He arrived in his wagon pulled by the team of horses and the plow loaded in the wagon. I was gone, and Joanne had not met him yet, but he came to the door and said, "Here is a pot of turkey stew. Would you put it on the stove and keep it warm 'til noon? Someone ran over the turkey, so I took it home and cooked it. This morning I put the mornings pancakes in it for dumplings." Joanne took the pot and put it on the stove. To say the least, it didn't look very appetizing with its brownish-gray color, and it gave off a bad odor all morning. When Mr. Cornet came to the house for dinner, he invited Joanne to eat with him, but she politely said she had already eaten lunch. I'm sure glad I wasn't home! He plowed an acre or more, did a good job, and only charged ten dollars for the days work.

I had one more meeting with the old man. An unexpected meeting. I was driving down Ranchito Road in Taos, crossing a bridge on a curve, when all at once a run-a-way team of horses came charging around the curve in the road, pulling a wagon. The horses were headed right for me and I was in the middle of the bridge, so as soon as I could get to the end of the bridge I headed the pickup for the ditch. It seemed like they just wanted to straddle the pickup and that is what they did, except their harness wouldn't let them get that far apart, so the larger horse went on one side of the pickup and pulled the other horse onto the top of the hood. I ducked down in the floorboard just as the tongue of the wagon hit the front of the hood. It looked like the tongue and the horses were coming in through the windshield. Finally the larger horse dragged the other horse off the hood and into the bar-ditch where the broken tongue stuck in the ground and stopped the team. I got out of the pickup . . . and calmed the horses down.

There was no driver in the wagon, so I figured they had thrown him out someplace down the road. I walked down the road and around the curve to see if I could find him. About a half mile away I saw old man Cornet walking toward me. When he finally got there, he explained that he had finished plowing a field and was leaving the field when he got off the wagon to close the gate. A truck had come by and scared his horses.

It didn't turn out too awfully bad, I guess. A little bodywork would fix the pickup, a new tongue was put on the wagon, some patchwork done on the harness, and everyone was ready to go again.

WILD CATTLE

Since we were raising Registered Angus Cattle, we decided to join the New Mexico State Angus Association. The main purpose of this was to market the bulls and heifers. The association had an annual meeting at Roswell, New Mexico with a banquet, western dance, Angus Show, and followed with a cattle sale.

The first year we took some yearling calves down there, we hadn't had much time to halter break them. We put halters on them at home and tied them in the trailer, so by the time we got to Roswell, they were getting sort of accustomed to the halters. When I untied one calf to lead it into the barn to the stalls, he took off with me just a hanging on. One old timer that was always at the show and sale for years after that used to say, "I remember the first time I saw old Bob. He was flying through the air, holding onto the end of a halter, with one of his calves on the other end."

Later on, one of my good friends from House, New Mexico, Byers Irwin, brought a pretty big, real nice heifer to the show. He hadn't gotten around to breaking her very good either, so he wasn't even going to show her. Then he thought, "If Bob is there I'll get him to show the wild heifer." I guess I was getting a reputation. Well, I was willing to try, and I took it real easy with the heifer. We made it fine, and I think she won reserve champion.

NICE LITTLE HEIFER

We had a heifer that we wanted to halter break and take to the State Fair in Albuquerque, NM. Whenever I roped her, she got really mad. I snubbed her to a tree until I could get a halter on her. It took a while, but I finally got the halter on her and kept her tied to the tree. By then she was so mad she just screamed, fell down, turned flips, and carried on worse than any animal I had ever worked with. I kept her tied most of the day, but she wouldn't calm down. I untied her to try to lead her, but there was no way could I hold onto her. She broke loose, jumped the corral fence, ran down the hill toward the creek, jumped our property fence and that was the last I saw of her.

I found her tracks along the creek bank several times, so I knew she was still between our place and town. One of our neighbors knew about the heifer getting away. One late night, he and his wife were driving home from town. They saw the heifer walking down the highway. He was a pretty good roper, and he had his rope with him, so he had his wife drive while he sat on the front fender of the pickup. When they got up close enough, he roped her, but there wasn't anything to snub to. He sure couldn't hold on to her otherwise, so he had to let go of the rope. I had lost my halter and then he lost his rope. A *new* rope at that!

The next time we heard of her about a week or so later.

She was about five miles down the canyon in an orchard. We were about the only family in the area that raised black cattle, so the word got back to us about the heifer. We took the pickup and trailer down to the orchard and backed it up to a gate in the fence. I hid behind an apple tree with my rope, while Joanne drove her along the rows of trees.

When she came by, I threw the loop and actually caught her! I had her caught, but she took off like a jet, and I wasn't fast enough to snub the rope around a tree. In a short time she slowed down and began walking the fence to find a good place to jump out. I slipped along through the trees and hid near where she would come by, then jumped out, grabbed the rope, ran up to the next tree and snubbed it before she knew what was happening. Well, now we had her caught good, but how would we get her to the trailer? Well, I threw another rope on her, Joanne took one rope and snubbed it to a tree while I moved up to the next tree and snubbed to it, until we had worked our way across the orchard to the trailer. Then we put one rope up through the front of the trailer and pulled her in. Finally, this big chore was over, what a great relief!

When we had her home again, I was determined to get her halter broke, so I worked with her every chance I got. By moving real slow and being very gentle, I had her calmed down and was able to lead her around a little. Time for the fair was coming up soon. We got to the fair with her, and there, we had about three days to work with her before the show. She was coming along pretty good!

The morning came for the Angus Show and my heifer's class. It was time to go into the show ring with my "nice little heifer". As long as I kept a good tight hold on the halter lead rope and moved with as much ease as I could, we made out all right through the class showing.

The heifer took second place, and I was pleased even though the class was not very big. Everything went real good until the Angus Queen stuck her hand out to give me the red ribbon. The heifer jumped and in a split second had turned, and headed for the other end of the show ring. I was barely able to hold on to the end of the halter, but luckily I did manage to get her stopped and under control again. I don't think it was the color of the ribbon that caused the outburst, but just the movement of the hand and the ribbon.

DETERMINATION

While I'm on the subject of showing cattle, I may as well tell about my trip to the Arizona National Livestock Show in Phoenix. The show was held on the first week of January, but I thought, being in Phoenix, it would be warm and I might even go swimming. That was not the case. When I left home the weather wasn't bad at all, so I was going to sleep in the front end of the gooseneck trailer with the cattle the first night because I would only be halfway there. I got to Show Low, Arizona, fed the cattle and crawled into my bedroll. The longer the night went, the colder I got. I lay there dosing and shivering all night long. When I got up at daylight, I discovered that it had snowed about six inches, and the cattle were covered with snow. I hurried around, fed them some hay and drove down to the first café I could find to get some breakfast and good hot coffee.

I thawed out and started on down the road but soon came to the Salt River Canyon. It is very winding and especially steep. The traffic that had passed earlier had packed the snow until it was a sheet of ice. I tried to go slow, but with no brakes on the trailer, when I'd put the brakes on in the pickup, the trailer would try to come around the pickup. When I geared the pickup down, the trailer with the load of show animals would still try to slide around the side of the pickup. On one side of the highway there was a thousand feet or so drop, and on the other side, the cliff rose straight up, so I sure tried to stay away from the downhill (cliff) side, even thought it was not my side of the highway. Finally, in spite of all I could do, the trailer came on around and crashed into the side of the pickup. We came to a stop when the pickup hit a highway sign. I was sure glad to be stopped! I bent the sign over some more so I could drive on over it and back to my own side of the highway. I did this very slowly, then put my tire chains on, which I should have *already* done. The chains helped a little although I still had to creep on down the road very slowly.

I couldn't seem to get warm at the fair grounds. It was freezing and the water pipes burst, so I did not do any swimming while there. I could hardly make myself work with the cattle. All I had for a coat was a Levi jacket, so I just wanted to stand in the sunshine and try to thaw out.

I had two bulls in a class of about twenty. I was able to find someone to help me show one of the bulls. I had bought two new halters, and so they weren't broke in and formed to the bull's heads. Out in the show ring I was trying to keep my eye on both my bulls and the judge. We were lined up and the judge was coming down the line. I looked down just in time to see the bull I was showing just sort of back right out of his halter. Right away, he realized he was free. Since he had been tied up for several days he took advantage of the situation and started running and bucking all over the show ring, which was so neatly covered with turquoise painted, saw dust. The pretty saw dust was flying all over. There were dignitaries in the show ring such as the American Angus Representative from St. Joseph, Missouri, the Arizona Angus President, and others. They helped me get the bull in a corner, and I eased up on him, threw the halter lead strap over his neck, reached down and grabbed it from underneath. I had him and I wasn't going to turn loose. I got the halter back on his head and led him back over to my place in the line up. The judge had already started placing the bulls. I think my two bulls got sixteenth and seventeenth place out of the twenty. I was very embarrassed, but pleased with the placing. After the show I met some friends of mine that had been watching the show. One of them said, "When you were about to catch that bull, you had the most determined look on your face I have ever seen!"

A STITCH IN TIME

We needed more grass for the cattle when a real good deal on ranch land, considering prices in the Taos area, came up in Las Cordovas. We managed to buy the land. The place was about two miles down stream from where three creeks came together to make a pretty good-sized river, the Rio Pueblo. The river ran through the north end of our new place. This was a perfect place to raise cattle. There was a good barn, fairly good corral, an old adobe house, and some good Vega, grass, land down by the river. The fences were not too good. As for most fences in Taos County, I don't think there were many good ones. We have spent about thirty years fixing other peoples fences and then we also had some of our own to fix.

The fence on the north divided our land from the Indian Reservation. It ran along the side of a very rocky and steep riverbank. Neither the last owners nor the Indians had spent much time fixing the fence in this area. I guess a good excuse was that it was so rough. Our cattle were beginning to get out on this end, so the first chance I had, I took some steel posts and a post driver down to the place to do a little fence mending. I had to wade and swim across the river to get to the bad place in the fence. Finally I got everything across the river and began putting the posts in the ground. I would put the 'driver' over the post, raise the post into position and begin driving the post into the hard, rocky ground. I had to hold the barbed wire away from the driver with my leg, so I could get a good solid lick, or strike with the driver. I must have let my leg relax, and the wire came in too close to the post. The driver caught the "bob wire" (as our family called barbed wire) and sent the wire down against my leg, tearing my Levis and making a big gash in my leg just above my knee. I was bleeding pretty good, so I took my handkerchief and tied it around my leg for sort of a pressure bandage.

Well, I still needed to get a couple more posts in, and I wanted to do it then so I wouldn't have to swim the river again later. I finished putting in the other posts, gathered my tools and swam back across the river. When I got out of the river on the other side, I looked like I had been wounded in the war. The blood and water really made the gash look much worse than it was.

When I got back home, up the Canyon, which was about twelve miles to drive, Joanne looked at me and said, "Let's go to the emergency room at the hospital and get you sewed up." I knew that would cost a lot of money, so I told her to just get a needle and thread and sew it up. She didn't want to do that *at all,* but I insisted. She finally put three or four stitches in the four-inch gash. Well, my leg healed up just fine.

Since then, Joanne has been known as 'Nurse Pringle', especially at family gatherings, and more especially when someone is hurt. Right away, we call for 'Nurse Pringle'!

The old adobe house on the place had an attic, which served as some upstairs bedrooms for some of the ten kids that were growing up there. Their mother, a widow, was trying to raise them on what they could make from a few head of sheep that they were able to raise on the grass that grew there. Her husband, and the father of the ten kids, had died not too long before of a gunshot. Some say it was from his own gun and that he had pulled the trigger. I'm sure his own gun killed him, but I'm not so sure that he was the one who pulled the trigger.

After we took possession of the place, the widow and all her kids continued to live in the house for some time because they had to wait for a new house to be built on another piece of property for them. They still had some sheep there and kept the place irrigated. This place was on the very end of the irrigation ditch line, so if it snowed a lot in the winter there would be enough water to get to the end of the ditch in the spring and make everyone else happy in the upper and middle part of the ditch, but if it didn't snow very much, there wasn't enough water to go around. The water would be used up before it got to the end of the ditch.

One day when I went out to 'the place' to check on the cattle, the widow and her kids were irrigating the meadow. There was plenty of water running everywhere and covering the meadow. The grass really looked good! I stopped to visit a little while and she told me she was raising those ten kids, and said, "I could raise ten more."

No one was living in the old house since the family had moved out. We had brought a few pieces of furniture and an old wood burning stove to the house. A temporary neighbor from the place southwest of us asked if he could stay in the house in exchange for doing some irrigating and work on the fence. This sounded like a good deal, so we let him move in.

I was going to be gone to Albuquerque, New Mexico for about a week or so, so Joanne was going to check on the cattle. We had not fixed the stovepipe very well, although it was placed through the ceiling and on through the roof. I guess this was on Joanne's mind. When she lay down to take a nap, she dreamed that the old house in Las Cordovas was burning down. She jumped up, grabbed the kids and hurriedly drove down to check on the place. Sure enough, when she got near she could see the smoke coming up over the hill. The fire truck came shortly afterward, but it was too late. The entire house had burned up except the four adobe walls. We should have told the old man not to build a fire in the stove, but we figured he had enough sense not to. Well, so much for the house, and me getting the irrigation and fencing done!

From this place in Las Cordovas, there was a great view in all directions, including a great view of the Sangre de Cristo Mountains. Who could ask for a better place to go fishing than right there? Well, we got an offer from some people to buy the place, and even though we didn't want to sell it, they kept making the offer better until I could not resist any longer. That is where I made one of my many mistakes, and this was one of the worst! We did sell the Las Cordovas Place. There we were, back to leasing pasture for the cattle, *and* fixing other people's fences again.

REUNION

It was a unanimous decision that there be a Caudle Family reunion in Trinidad, Colorado, out at the Gray Creek Road Place. This was going to be a big blowout.

When time for the reunion was getting near, several of the family members came early to help get the place ready. We painted, cleaned, built a carport that would also serve as a shady place out doors to gather, laid a brick sidewalk, and built a fence between the house and corral, and numerous other things. Relatives began gathering and planning a very interesting schedule of events.

During a rest time, the men sat out in the shade of some cedar trees. One of Daisy's son-in-laws, sat, chewed tobacco, spit, whittled, and told some old tales. He was getting on up in years. All at once he said, "You know, I wouldn't give you a dime for this whole place, you can't see a cow no where." The reason you couldn't see a cow was that they were lying under the trees in the shade, and the place was about half covered with pinion and cedar trees. He was used to running cattle in the God forsaken open country of Southeastern Colorado. We told Daisy what he had said. She indignity exclaimed, "Did you tell him it isn't for sale!?"

The next day, the windmill needed a little work done on it. We gathered up some tools and went down to the well. The same son-in-law came along. This had been a hand dug well about twenty-eight feet deep, so I was lowered down to the bottom with a rope to do some work. I think I had to put some new 'leathers' on the bottom check. We had to pull the pipe up out of the water a ways. When we tried to lower it back down again, we were sort of off to the side of the well and it didn't go all the way down. Then we moved it over more to the other side and it went down to the right depth with ease. I also fixed the sucker rod just above the pipe where it was about to wear in two. I did this with what little I had there to work with, kind of temporary. We finally got it ready to pump water again. All this time, the older son-in-law never said a word, just watched, and he probably knew more about fixing windmills than all of us put together. When we got back to the house, someone asked the son-in-law if we had gotten the windmill fixed, and he said, "Yeow, 'bout half-assed." Joanne asked the Son-in-law if there was any water in the well. He answered, "Yeow, but there's more water on one side of the well than on the other." Everyone got some laughs and fun from that one! I guess that's part of having a good time and a great reunion!

OUTHOUSES

It was suggested earlier that at the same gathering, we should have an outside privy. There was still one there at the place but it hadn't been used in years, except in necessities, and might not stand up through the 'rush', so I offered to bring another one. This was to keep some of the 'people traffic' out of the house, since there would be lots of other activities going on in there.

The story about this certain outhouse goes back several years. A building contractor left it in Red River, NM on a building site, and I was told I could have it if I would haul it away. So one weekend Joanne and I went to Red River and loaded the outhouse on the back of the old pickup we owned and were driving at the time. The pickup had been owned by one of the past Taos Mayors and looked like it had been in a few too many wine-drinking parties. Anyway, on the way out of Red River, Joanne slid down between the dash and the seat, so no one could see her. I saw some friends of ours out in their yard. They were rather 'well to do' and owned a business there. I said, "Let's stop and say, 'Hello'." But Joanne didn't want me to stop or for them to even see us. She *wanted* me to keep right on driving. So *of course,* I stopped and we had a little visit. The whole time Joanne was so embarrassed she almost died. But she got over it. After we got the outhouse home, it sat without being used for some time. Then a lady named, Dell bought the place to the West of us. She was going to build a house, but they needed to borrow our outhouse until they got the house built. I hauled it over to 'Dell's Half Acre', and it stayed there for several years.

ANGUS FIELD DAY

We were pretty involved in the Angus business by that time and it was our turn to host the Annual Angus Field Day. We expected a large crowd of people from all over New Mexico, Texas, and Colorado. It was the usual thing to have an outside privy or two, so I had to take some time out from fixing up the place, to go get the outhouse from Dell's back yard. It had been many years since anyone had driven into her place. Some young trees had grown up in the road, which was a pretty steep drive into where the outhouse was. I parked the pickup at the top of the hill while we cleared the road. Martin and I were busy clearing the trees when we heard something strange. We looked up and it was the pickup coming down the hill. We had to run to get out of the way. The pickup crashed into some trees and kept it from going into the creek, which was pretty deep at that point. I had left it in gear, but the engine compression wasn't enough to hold the pickup on the hill. I *should* have put a rock in front of the wheel. Anyway, we had to get a wrecker to come out and pull the pickup out. Then we proceeded to load the outhouse and take it home.

One day before the field day, the New Mexico Angus President and his wife came to see if they could be of any help getting things ready. I told him he could put some 'His and Hers' names on the outhouses. (We already had one sitting here idle.) We have a picture of the Angus President putting the names on the outhouses. He made a statement later at the ceremony, saying, "The only thing Bob thought I was capable of doing was to clean and fix up the out-houses." Our Angus Field Day was a success. We didn't have any big catastrophes, and we didn't get rained out. So everything went well.

CAUDLE
REUNION–CONTINUED

In a few days we were to have the reunion at Trinidad, so we had to get that outhouse over there. Joanne, Martin, Regan, and I loaded it in the pickup along with some other things to work with, and headed out. When we arrived there, it was decided that the best place for it would be down by the corral near some pinion trees. While trying to unload it, it got away from us and toppled out. That outhouse got one more 'lick' in on me when it caught my arm, and ripped a pretty good gash in it. "Time to get 'Nurse Pringle' again!"

It was about time for the reunion crowd to arrive so we needed to get back to the fixing up, painting, nailing boards, and all.

I tried my best to keep my son, Regan, busy but his cousin, Randy, was not at all interested in working, in fact I don't think he knew what the word meant. So he kept taking Regan off away from the work, and keeping me very upset.

At the same time, though, Regan was teaching Randy how to dip snuff. I forgot to mention that they were about ten or eleven years old, and Regan was already an old hand at dipping. Needless to say, these lessons weren't setting to well with Randy's grandmother, or his mother. Now, fifteen years later, they're still blaming us for the big dentist bills!

Not really!! I hope!!!

GOOD EDUCATION

As we increased the size of our Angus herd each year, we also tried to improve the quality. In 1972 we had the Grand Champion Heifer and the Grand Champion Bull at the New Mexico Angus Show and Sale at Roswell. This was a great honor, and we brought home some nice trophies.

I was the vice-president, and then our president died, so that put me in the President's place. This was something that I had never even dreamed of becoming. One never knows what can happen and what the future will bring! At this particular time the president's job was not too popular of a position, that is, I don't think very many of the members wanted the job, because two of our other presidents before the last one had died also. Well, I made it *alive* through the term and was elected for another term. Joanne was also elected President of the Ladies Angus Auxiliary, and then we were elected to go to Chicago to the National Convention as delegates from New Mexico. That was another big honor. We flew from Albuquerque to Chicago. The plane didn't even crash!

On the way home, we did have a little misunderstanding when we got back on the plane from a stop. Some gal and her kid had taken our seats, which we had plainly marked before we got off. The stewardess took the gal's side and made us find other seats. So I sat and steamed the rest of the way. When the gal and her kid got up at the last stop, there were our 'seat taken' signs right where we had left them. They had been sitting on them all the time. I wanted to run, catch up with them, and . . . and . . . and . . . get even!

We never did win a Grand Champion prize at the State Fair, although we have tried for several years. The kids have won their share of trophies at the New Mexico State Fair in the junior division, so that makes up for our loss.

Anyway we have done pretty well with our cattle. We were even mentioned in a little book written by an old rancher from up on the plains of New Mexico. The name of the book is, *Where The Coyote Howls.* In the book he mentioned some top horse breeders in the state, then went on to say, "There is a list of Angus and Hereford breeders that have worked extra hard to improve the breed of cattle, and they are:" He named several Angus breeders from up on the plains and around Tucumcari, and then; Bob Mead of Taos, New Mexico.

The article mentioned that I was educated in House, New Mexico, and had done remarkably well for a young man with a lot of ambition.

Above all, it was a real compliment to have gotten my education at House, NM!

RENTERS

This story happened in the summer of 1988, I think. Henry and Daisy were both gone to the Great Divide. Joanne and I ended up buying the rest of her folks' place on Gray Creek Road from her other sisters. They felt since we already owned part of the place, we should buy the rest of it. Then we had a house to live in when we went to Trinidad, or we could rent it out. We also had more grass to run the cattle on.

The price of gas was so high, and there would be a lot of running back and forth, so we choose to rent out both the house and the pasture. In fact we have rented it out for some time now and we have had some real "Jim Dandies".

One renter woman made herself at home to the whole ranch, going around gathering old relics, and arrowheads. We don't know what all she got off with. We were glad to get rid of her only because the basement had waterdogs and other slimy things in it. This was because she was too lazy to ditch the rainwater away from the house, so it wouldn't run into the basement. I don't think we ever got paid for the last two months of rent.

The next outfit must have had a fight and split up. Anyway, they took off for Missouri in such a hurry, they left most of their junk scattered all over the house and yard. They left a car that we had to sell and we're still selling the other stuff in yard sales when we get the chance, you know for a dime or a quarter—big money.

The next renter had a good job and paid the rent, but never cleaned the house as long as they lived there, I'm sure. We went to see how they were getting along one time, and the lady had a mop bucket out with a mop standing in it. She said she was cleaning house, which could have counted for the dirt and everything being in such a state of disaster. Well, a month and a half later they moved out and left most of their things scattered all around. That mop bucket was still sitting in the same place. The water had dried up with the mop still stuck solid to the bottom of the bucket.

It was on this house-cleaning trip that I came to help. Joanne and I had pretty well gotten the house back in shape, but it was late and we decided to spend the night. We made a pallet on the floor in the bedroom, and when it got dark we went to bed because the electricity had been turned off.

Well, about midnight or so, I heard what sounded like several motorcycles coming up the road, and then stop out by the front gate, which is about fifty yards from the house. There they sat with their machines idling. I rose up in bed and listened for a second, thinking it must be about a dozen hoodlums. I woke Joanne up and told her to hurry, get up, and get her clothes on. At the same time I was trying to get my clothes on, and looking for the flashlight. I could imagine about ten or so big hippie type guys with leather jackets plotting to raid the house, and all.

We went to the door to look out, there was no moon at all, so it was pitch black out there. The driveway was graveled, and we could hear the crunch, crunch, crunch of footsteps coming up the graveled driveway, although the footsteps didn't seem to be getting much closer.

Finally Joanne said, "That's a cow." And sure enough it was, biting off bits of the old dry grass. We had leased the pasture to an old family friend, and he had several head of cows in there. There hadn't been any rain, so the grass was so dry it made a real crunching noise every time the cow took a bite. Well, we got 'brave' and went outside to meet the 'cows' face to face.

Now, you are probably wondering about the motor-cycles. Well, when we were outside, we realized the sound was coming from town, about two and a half miles away. Then we could tell the noise had been a diesel train pulling into the terminal and was sitting there with the engines running, or idling, "burummm, burummm, burummm".

Well, I'll never live *that* one down! It was still hard to get back to sleep even though there were no motorcycles.

TAOSENOS

I didn't know 'Spud' very well, and I don't know much about him, except that he was part of the Art Circle around Taos, and that he was a columnist writer for the Taos newspaper 'El Crepusculo'. Many of his articles were about keeping Taos as it was, against large signs, neon signs, and for buildings to be only the kind that would be suitable to the territory. The sketch on the opposite page was done of me by 'Spud' while I was working on some telephone trouble at the news office. It came out in the local paper, and I've kept it for forty-five years. Now I think it appropriate to put it in this book.

Spud lived in a little house between El Prado and Taos on the bank of the El Pueblo Creek. He has been dead for several years, and now his old place is a bed and breakfast, called "The Laughing Horse", named after a magazine Spud had published years ago.

Spud was bald headed, and wore many different kinds of hats. At times he was known to wear a wig, and other times he didn't, so he was also known as, "The man who scalps himself."

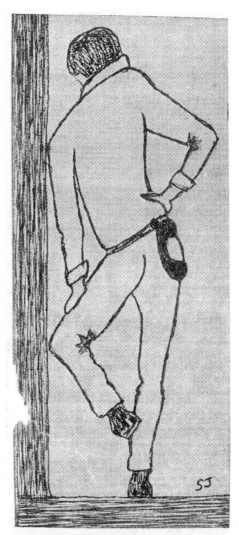

One leg propped against the other in a precarious pose that suggests deep thought, a telephone company line-man mulls over difficult electronic problems following customer's complaint.

TAOS FRIENDS
PAT

Another Taos friend, Pat, was an Indian from the Pueblo. I met him not long after we had moved to Taos. It got so I would have to dodge Pat because he usually would want a quarter to buy some wine.

Pat could plaster a little, in fact he had helped build the house that we live in now. We had him come to plaster the backside of the old adobe barn, which had never been plastered. The adobes were just like they were the day they were put up, except where snow had piled up next to them, and then melted in the spring. The water was beginning to melt the adobes away. The barn was about twenty years old by then. We had Pat come in at noon to eat with us, and he talked about the tourists, and the silly questions they asked such as, "What do you eat for breakfast?"

Pat didn't say what he had answered them, so I asked, "What *do* you eat for breakfast?" And he said, "Bacon an' eggs".

TONY

Tony was another Indian friend. He was more of a cowboy than most of the other Indians, and he worked outside of the Pueblo, mostly on ranch jobs

When Tony would see me in town near the Plaza, he would detain me for a good while, saying, "Hello, Baub, my frien', you know me, an' I know you, an' you know me, an' I know you Baub, an' can I tell you a story?" So the story would be a long story about him and Billy The Kid, or something like that. Before he would let me go on my way, he would say, "Baub, my frien', I like you, and you like me, an' could you help me with a dollar?"

Tony liked Joanne real well, because she rode his horse in a horse race and won. He was really proud of both his horse and Joanne! From then on, he called Joanne his 'Jockey Girlfriend'. Tony would say, "I like you, Joanne. Joanne, you're *my* Jockey!"

Our friend Chet hired Tony to do ranch or cowboy type work, or just have Tony along for company. Chet teased Tony at times. He was teasing Tony about his girlfriend that lived in the Canyon, Joanne. So Tony answered back, "Aw Chat, You jus' jelly!"

On one meeting with Tony, he said, "Hallo Baub, I know you and you know me and you know Chat, and you know Baub, Chat is mat with me. I been stayin' in his bunk house, an you know Baub, Chat throw my bed roll out, and my saddle out, and tell me to leave." His sad story was much longer, and told over and over.

RANCHITO

On the outskirts of Taos, there is a little community called Ranchitos. We found some pasture there for our cattle, and kept it leased for several years. It was handy to get to and the grass grew pretty good as part of it was subirrigated.

There were some disadvantages to it, too. There was a county road running past the place on each end, and there was always some kind of vehicle running through the fence. If I didn't catch the person that ran through the fence before they drove out and away, or the wrecker towed them away, or the neighbors found out who it was, I never could find out who did it.

There was no one to rebuild the fence, except the family and me. We have been called in the middle of the night many times to go down and fix the fence because someone had driven through it. This usually happened on Friday or Saturday nights, the night of some kind of celebration, Christmas Eve, or New Year's Eve. We should have put in a fence building business!

Anyway, to get to what this story is all about.

Some neighbors, who lived on up the canyon, had bought a few head of Registered Angus Cattle from us. They were excited about their new herd, and wanted to talk or read anything they could find about cattle.

They ran across an article, which was an excerpt from a book that had been published. The article told about a bunch of cattle that were in the pasture next door to where the author of the book lived. Well, they thought this was the funniest story they had ever read, and couldn't wait for us to read it.

I read part of the story, and then asked them who had written the story. They said a writer that lived down on Ranchito Road. I said, "I thought so, because I had heard that a writer lived next to our pasture, but we had never met him."

Well, I didn't think the story was so funny, because it sounded too much like our pasture and cattle. We did find out that our cattle had been getting out and we didn't know it, because the neighbor would just put them back in the pasture and halfway fix the fence but not say anything to us about it.

The story went something like this:

"We were awakened in the middle of the night by the screeching noise of the ancient barbed wire fence being stretched beyond its limit and the snap of brittle old cedar posts. This was the fence that had been between my lush green yard and garden and the dry, overgrazed pasture next door where a bunch of hungry Angus cattle were kept. The cattle were stretching their necks through the fence and leaning against the old wires, until the fence gave in.

Cattle were in my yard, walking over the doghouse, urinating on my Volkswagen bus, chewing on the jockey shorts that hung on the line, stepping on the kid's bicycles, and other toys, and eating the limbs off the young orchard trees. I had to get up, take some tranquilizer pills and herd this bunch of cattle back into their pasture. Then I attempted to mend the fence with a flashlight."

I wrote a letter to John Nichols apologizing for the trouble my cattle had been to him.

Dear John,
Some time ago, some neighbors of mine bought a few head of Angus cattle from me. This being their first cattle to own, they were very enthusiastic about cattle and wanted to read or talk about cattle in general. They happened to get hold of the 'Taos Magazine' with some excerpts from your book, *If Mountains Die*. My friends

thought the story was so funny that on their next visit, they told me about the story. It sounded familiar, so I asked who wrote the story, and they gave your name. I said, "Oh, I see, he lives next to our pasture." Then they had to read the story again and thought it even funnier. Next visit, they brought the magazine for me to read. It is very funny (now) and yet rather embarrassing that I had not taken better care of my cattle and the pasture.

The reason for this letter, I suppose is to apologize for the damage my cattle did to your property and your nerves. To think back, you never did complain. There are some old bicycles around here you may have if yours are still in need of repair. If your rose bushes haven't come out of it yet, maybe I can give you another start.

Since the banker has now bought the place next door and built that monstrous house between you and the mountains, I sometimes wonder if you wouldn't rather have the cattle back in the 'overgrazed pasture', or maybe not.

I had not read any of your books before now, but have just finished, *The Milagro Beanfield War.* It's a very good book and most descriptive. I'll be getting your book, *If Mountains Die,* soon. Please accept my apology and my offer to make 'good' the damage.

Sincerely,
Bob Mead

I had no idea that John Nichols would do anything but glance at my letter and throw it in the waste paper basket, but to my surprise, in a few days I received the following reply. By the way it started out, I thought he was pretty mad. It read:

Dear Mr. Mead:
Nope, I don't need any bicycles or new rose bushes; but many thanks for your generous and thoughtful letter offering it. From a purely technical point of view, I've always known that the New Mexico law read you got to fence cattle out, rather than expecting others to fence them in, and of course, I have always fenced 'em out like everybody else—that is, I collect bailing wire like it was gold,

and patch my fence as if it were a ragamuffin's britches. So of course, it never really holds. I've figured that in dealing with one's neighbor's horses, cows, dogs, cats, peacocks, at all is just one of those things that goes along with living in Taos—it's part of the frustration and part of the charm. And you're right of course; I'd rather have your cantankerous cattle in Phil Lavidie's field than that enormous house. Even if those cattle may at times have bugged me, I always felt a nice personal emotional involvement with them, and liked having them around when I wasn't cursing them. They were beautiful in their own way, too. I always liked to watch them, especially in snowstorms, or listen to them bellowing at night.

That new, huge house is pretty impersonal, mighty cold. If it weren't for various animal intruders, who knows I might not even be able to make a living. One of my more famous characters from *The Milagro Beanfield War,* Pig, came about directly from a few encounters I had with an enormous sow belonging to one Alfredo Pacheco, I believe. Anyway, he used to live beside that small Campo Santo on the Middle Road near the old town dump. One day, he brought his sow over to my neighbors, the Mondragons, to breed her with their bore. She escaped, wondering over to my place, and destroyed my beautiful garden. I could have killed her—instead she almost killed me! Then about half an hour later, along came Pacheco himself, looking for her. I invited him in for a drink, and we got to playing the guitar together and talking. Later his sow, and himself, in fact, became central figures in the *Beanfield War,* and, in fact, the fictional death of the pig became one of the bearings upon which the (admittedly loose) plot turned. So all clouds have equally wonderful silver linings. Which isn't to say I didn't go around like crazy a week ago when a whole herd of whiteface Herefords came marching into my front field just after Tom Trujillo had cut it, but before he had bailed it! Nor that I didn't shed many a tear and curse my neighbor's dogs when they killed all my rabbits last autumn. But, you know, that's life. It comes with the territory, and helps make the territory vital and exciting as well as tragic.

My for heaven's sake, feel no guilt over the past depredations of your cows. Look at it this way, you earn a living from your cattle, and in a way so have I, by writing about my adventures with them in *If Mountains Die.* I mean, I should thank you for all their incursions onto my territory. Thanks for reading *Milagro.* And special thanks for taking the time to send that letter.

Sincerely,
John Nichols

Well, then I felt much better about the whole problem. We did try harder to keep our cattle at home.

NAMES

For some reason in 1961, Henry and Daisy, Joanne's folks wanted to sell us another eighty acres next to the eighty we had bought in 1954. I had made *another* big mistake and sold our nice herd of Angus Cattle we had built up, to a man with lot of talk and a big wad of money in his pocket. (But that is too disturbing to talk about, and no humor in it.) Anyway, it was time to get back into the business, so we bought ten pair of mixed cows and calves to put on the land at Trinidad.

Not being able to get away from being an Angus breeder, we bought another Angus bull to put with them. The next spring, Joanne's sister, Maxine, was living with their mother on the Gray Creek Place. They had lots of fun watching the cattle and giving them some hay when the ground was covered with snow and the cattle couldn't graze.

At least it sounded as though they were having fun by the sound of the letters and they sent. The cows started calving. Most of the calves were black since their mothers were part black and their father was Black Angus. Maxine and Daisy had a thrill drawing pictures of each calf and naming them. Examples of the names were Tar Baby, Black Joe, and so on.

SUNDAY NO-NO'S

Last Sunday, we were in Sunday school, when the teacher was making a point about things we do in these modern days that have just begun to be accepted. Back several years ago, it was against the rules to do these things, and *for sure not done on a Sunday!*

This reminded me of when I was a kid in high school. I had a 1936 Ford Coupe. There was a good show on at the theatre in Melrose, thirty-five miles away. My cousin and I decided to go to the movie on a Sunday afternoon. We had been to church that morning, but it was still a no-no to go to a picture show on Sunday. Well, before we got there, the engine in my car started knocking and before we knew what had happened, a rod came through the block. My cousin said, "I knew we shouldn't have come over here on a *Sunday!*"

Everyone in the class thought that was a real funny story. It is one of those times I will never forget.

A BOARD ON THE HEAD

When the calves were about six to eight months old, it was about October, and time to wean the calves from their mothers. We gathered the calves and took them to the place in Taos Canyon. We kept them in the corral for about a week before we turned them out. Otherwise, the calves would find some way to get through the fence and try to find their way back to their mothers, even though they were eight or ten miles away.

We kept the calves in the canyon until they were about a year or two old. Then the bulls were sold as herd sires and the heifers were sold as replacement heifers for someone's herd. We kept the bulls in one pen and heifers in another, of course.

When Gaylynn, our daughter, was small she used to spend a lot of time working with me in the barn, working with the animals in the corral, fixing fence, or getting the animals halter broke in hopes that we could show them at the state fair, or take them to the Show and Sale in Roswell, New Mexico.

One time when Gaylynn was about five years old. The two of us were catching bulls that were about a year old. One of the bulls was pretty ornery and would run at a person to try to knock them down if they didn't get out of the way or hit the bull with something. I told Gaylynn that if the bull started toward her, she should hit him over the head with the short 2×4 board I had given her. Well, sure enough, the bull saw his chance to go after her, and just before he reached her, I hollered, "Hit 'em!" Gaylynn just kept her feet planted right there and came down with a mighty blow as she broke the board on the bull's head. He came to a sliding stop and looked at her as if he couldn't believe what had happened, then he turned and ran the other way. Gaylynn must have had a lot guts to stand there like that!

SAD GOODBYE

We were raising bulls and heifers to sell as registered animals for someone's herd bull or heifers to put in their herd or to start a new herd. I usually had several in the corral for sale. My daughter, Gaylynn, was the first of the three kids to start a 4-H project with one of these bulls. She and I spent a lot of time in and around the corral working with all the animals, including hers, and getting them ready to show at the county fair and then at the State Fair.

One day a bull buyer came by the place to look at bulls, and when he had looked at them all, he decided on one of my bulls, and Gaylynn's bull. Rather than disappoint the buyer, and take a chance on loosing the sale, I insisted she sell him her bull. I didn't know that she was as attached to the bull, as she must have been. I knew she didn't want to sell him, but we loaded him up anyway, and then the tears begin to flow. The buyer noticed the tears, and then they became sobs. I'm sure he hated to drive off with her bull.

Several weeks later, when the man was back in our part of the country, he stopped by the house and gave Gaylynn a nice blue calf halter. I think she may have had another calf to use it on by that time. I don't know if this made her feel better or not, and maybe the buyer didn't think he had done enough to make up for the hurt, yet, so, the next time he came by our place, he brought her a brand new whip to work cattle with.

That must have been the end of the gifts. He and his wife became friends and also came to our Angus Field Day.

GET THAT GATE!

In Taos Canyon where we live, sound travels pretty far and clear, especially when everything is calm and quiet.

I have done my share of yelling at the three kids and Joanne, especially when we are working with the cattle. When I'm yelling, I don't care how far the sound travels, or who hears me. (We *were* the first to live in this area!)

We had some neighbors down the canyon a short ways who had a few horses. One day he was over at our house and reminded me about how voices carry in the canyon. One day he was out working with his horses when he heard me yell, "Get that gate!" He said he jumped and looked all around for the gate he needed to close. We had probably left a gate open; the bulls had gotten out, and were headed for another gate that was open, or something like that.

Things like that, or something else, were happening all the time, usually when we were in a hurry to go someplace. So of course all the animals would get out and head down the road to our neighbors garden, one direction or the other. When we got home, we would usually have a report from someone with all the details of how hard it was to get our cattle and horses back into the pasture or corral where they belonged.

THERE SHE GOES!

One day, while we were working around the place here in the canyon, probably doing some spring clean up. We needed to back the pickup out of the garage. Martin said he would back it out for me, and since I had shown him a few things about driving, and he had practiced them, I told him to go ahead and back it out. He backed the pickup out, parked, got out, and then said, "Hey Dad, I just figured something out!"

About the time he said that, the pickup started rolling down the hill, and no one was close enough to stop it. The pickup *could* have missed hitting anything and ended up down in the meadow, but there happened to be the electric pole with a down-guy anchored right there in the way. The pickup hit the down-guy and caused the power pole to snap into three pieces with sparks flying all around. The pole to our transformer was on it, so of course, it came tumbling down too. The electric wires serving the transformer from across the canyon also came down and shorted out so *everyone living in the canyon* was without electricity.

We looked the situation over, and hated to call the power company, but there was no other choice. Men from Kit Carson Electric came out and spent the rest of the day removing all the broken stuff, and replacing the pole and transformer. The men finally finished up about midnight that night.

I never did know what it was that Martin had 'figured out', but I think he *may* have also figured out the need to leave a vehicle in gear, and the brake on when parking, especially on a hillside such as where we live.

TICKLED

Have you ever gotten tickled when you were in a place that you couldn't or shouldn't laugh, say . . . church? I sure have! The more I tried not to laugh, the more I needed to laugh. I have just about busted a gut trying to hold the laughter in!

When I was about eight or nine years old, I was sitting in church with my friend Marvin. Of course my Grandma was sitting not too far away in a pew behind us. Well, in came a fairly large lady with a very large bosom. Marvin said, "My goodness gracious! I'll bet she could sit her dinner plate on her bosom and eat dinner!" Well, that did it. The rest of the hour was pure misery. If it hadn't been for the songs, when we could let out some laughter and not be heard I think we would have died!

Joanne and I were sitting in front of a man and friend of ours on one particular Sunday morning. He liked to sing but I guess he was tone deaf because all the sounds of each word came out the same and with a real loud,

rough, gravelly voice at that. We both stopped singing just to listen to him for a while. Then we got tickled, and couldn't keep from laughing for the rest of the service. I guess he must have thought we were crazy, or had never been taught how to be reverent in church. We're sorry Ed!

One time the Preacher's Wife and another lady, who usually sat together in church, got tickled at the beginning of the morning service. They laughed through the entire service. I don't know if anyone knew what they were laughing about, and of course they tried not to let it show, but before the service was over, I think everyone was watching them instead of listening to the preacher. I wonder if he scolded her when they got home. That is, if preachers do scold their wives.

Both Joanne's Mother and my Mother came to Taos, NM for our oldest son, Martin's, graduation from Taos High School. Both Grandmothers sat next to each other. The person to be the main speaker at the graduation ceremony was Governor Anaya. (Some folks called him "Gov. Annoya".) He gave a very long-winded speech during which he talked and talked and talked.

Finally, Joanne's Mother, Daisy, said, "I wish he would just *shet up!*"

I had never seen or heard my Mother, Lillie, get so tickled! She sat there quietly shaking with laughter while tears ran down her cheeks. Ohhh, the pain!

MORE ABOUT SAVING

Folks who grew up during the Great Depression of the 1930's know about saving and learned to save in many unique and different ways.

After our family put *indoor* plumbing in the house, we quit using the Ward's Catalogue as toilet paper, and began using the store bought kind, which cost money. Everyone was required to do his or her part in being careful not to use too much. I found that I could do the job with just a *very few* sheets, and that became a habit which is still in effect today.

We seldom have trouble with our toilet stopping up and flowing over, when we are the only two using it, but it seems when we have company, that is when the toilet will overflow, and we'll have to use the plunger.

On one occasion, we had company, (family) and sure enough, right away, the toilet overflowed, so I did what was necessary to get it in working order again. It was then that I found a big wad of paper that had caused the problem, so I decided to give my thoughts on using toilet paper. A person only needs to use three sheets of toilet paper, and not a great big wad of paper. My sister-in law said, "*Why bother?!*" They haven't been to see us in a long time, so I may have hurt their feelings. I hope not.

Well, I'll have to take part of that judgment back. It has a lot to do with the quality of paper purchased. Joanne bought some cheap stuff the other day. A person has to use more than several sheets to do the job with that!

We were at a bull sale the other day, and the bulls sold for an average of nearly three thousand dollars a head. I was talking to well-known twin brothers after the sale. I mentioned the cheapest bull sold for eighteen hundred dollars. One of them said, "And that bull was the highest priced bull sold," meaning for what the buyer got. That is the way with cheap paper. It cost more than the highest priced paper you can buy.

Last April 1st, April Fool's Day, I had been complaining about the cheap toilet paper. Well, I noticed Joanne had replaced the 'cheap toilet paper' with an old roll of adding machine paper I had thrown away. We got a good laugh out of her April Fool's joke on me. That adding machine paper would have, maybe, worked better than the cheap stuff!

FISHING

One Easter, the first year Chris and Gaylynn were married and very financially stretched, the family gathered at our place in the canyon for a get-together. Before everyone had arrived, Martin and Chris, our son-in-law decided to go fishing. Chris, being an avid fisherman, and Martin not living where he could do much fishing, started out trying to catch a fish in the Rio Fernando Creek, or Taos Creek, that runs through our place. They were not having much luck, so decided to go down to the Rio Grande. They knew there were fish there.

It seems that neither one gave any thought of needing a fishing license when they took off. They were so engrossed with their fishing that when a Game Warden tapped Chris on the shoulder, he was pretty well shocked. While Chris was explaining that he was from Colorado, and didn't have New Mexico fishing license, he looked past the Warden to see Martin catch a fish and dangle it in the air showing it off to Chris. He shook the fish off his line just before the Warden turned to check Martin for his license, which he did not have either. Luckily, they hadn't caught any fish, the Warden said, or the fines would have been doubled.

The warden then informed the two of them that under New Mexico law he was supposed to handcuff them and haul them in to jail, but he was going to be nice about it and trust them to drive their own vehicle to the courthouse before being put in jail. The Warden then asked," who's going to make their one phone call?" Martin said," I'm not calling!" So Chris called the house to tell us they were in jail for fishing without a license.

Chris was already known for pulling Joanne's leg from time to time and had a heck of a time convincing her that they really were in jail, and that they needed help bad!

Gaylynn was very mad, but drove on down to the courthouse. She hauled Chris and Martin 'over the coals' so badly in front of all the jailhouse personnel, that the Warden and the Sheriff felt so sorry for Chris and Martin, they let them out of jail by only paying a large fine and did not require Chris to make the seven hundred mile return trip to Taos a week later to attend Court.

Chris thought he would never be able to go fishing or live that one down again, but I think he might have seen where her bad temper paid off that time.

ONLY ONE STEAK

After Martin, our oldest son had finished high school, a job seemed to be the next best thing in line, and around Taos, NM jobs were not always so easy to find.

We had bought a place down south of Tucumcari, and had put some cattle on it. One winter we got a neighbor to feed the cattle for us, and we bought the feed from him, so that worked out real well. He was going to need to hire some farm hands in the spring and summer, so I mentioned that Martin was a good worker and might want to work for him. He said to bring him down and he would give him a job with room and board. I told Martin about the job. He was real interested so we took him down to get him settled in with his new boss and job. They had to do numerous jobs, such as repair all kinds of machinery and farm equipment, get the ditches ready to run irrigation water, get the ground ready for planting, plant the crops, and so there was no end to the work, as with all farm and ranch work. I think they treated Martin pretty good and he was learning a lot, although he was working hard and the hours were long.

At supper one night the wife had most of the food on the table when Martin came in and sat down at the table while she was cooking the steak. She put one big steak on a platter in the middle of the table, and Martin, being very hungry, I guess, and thinking it was time to eat, forked the steak over on his plate and began eating. The boss and his wife got to the table, but there was no steak left for them!

The big steak was to have been divided among the three of them. Well, I don't know what happened next, but I suppose the wife went to the freezer and got another steak to cook for the two of them, I hope.

We tried to raise the kids to have some manners, and I think a few did rub of on them, but when you are real hungry, you might not remember them *all!*

RODEO BULLS

When Regan, our youngest of three, was in his high school years, he was pretty involved with High School Rodeo. He went to all of the high school rodeos around the state, and then at the end of the season, to the state rodeo finals. At this particular time and place, he needed a new hat. Joanne had given him money to buy one, with the understanding that he wouldn't wear it when he was riding a bull. We went to the western wear store, and Regan bought himself a thirty dollar straw hat. Later that day when it was Regan's turn to ride the bull he drew, he couldn't resist wearing that new hat.

Those rodeo bulls were as big and bad as the ones in the big time rodeo, in my opinion. Well, Regan came out of the chute on one big ole' bull. He rode him to the whistle, then was thrown to the ground and kicked in the head. Regan just lay there.

A friend of mine and I were sitting in the stand, and he said, "Don't you think we should go down and see about him?" I said, "Naw . . . he'll get up in a little bit." But pretty soon I began to get a 'little' worried because he wasn't getting up. We went down to the arena to see about him. All the other cowboys had already gathered around Regan, and had turned him over on his back. The blood from the hole in his head had run down around his neck and made a little pool of blood in the lower part of his throat. Some of the blood had run into his mouth. The snuff he was using, mixed together with the arena dirt made a terrible mess around his mouth.

Well, anyway he was beginning to want to get up, but the officials wouldn't let him. They wanted him to wait for the ambulance and attendants. The ambulance was there, but no one could find the keys to it, so another one was called from town about twelve miles away. I'm not sure if the ambulance ever got there, but I finally ended up taking him to the hospital myself. He eventually got to the hospital, where they cleaned him up and sewed up the hole in his head. Regan had another bull to ride that night, so we grabbed something to eat and went back to the rodeo grounds.

By the way, that new thirty-dollar straw hat looked like a piece of waste paper that had been wadded up to throw in the trash. He never did wear the hat again. The worst news was, when the bull riding started that night, they announced that Regan had gotten no score on that big bull because he had touched him with his free hand.

The rodeo hands and cowboys were pretty surprised to see him back, ready to ride his next bull that night.

FORGIVE AND FORGET

I don't remember why I didn't know better than to loan my pickup to my youngest son, Regan, but I do know I *should* have known better. Well, he did it to me again. Regan asked to use my pickup. For reason of softness, forgetfulness, forgiveness, or something else, I gave my permission.

He came home a little earlier than usual, but even at that it was late and we were in bed trying to get some sleep. He said, "Mom, I'm home." And "Dad, something is wrong with the pickup, it stalled at the gate and won't start."

The temperature was about zero, but I got out of my warm bed, got dressed, walked down the snow-covered driveway with a flashlight to the entrance of our place just off the highway. Sure enough it wouldn't start. The battery was too weak to turn the engine over. That was real strange. Could he have given someone a boost with the battery and gotten the leads reversed? No telling. I walked back up the hill to get another vehicle and some booster cables. The pickup started all right, but right away began steaming and screaming. It looked as if the battery was boiling. I had to get it to the house in a hurry before it burned up.

We took the battery out and sat it in the snow so it wouldn't explode. It still seemed to be boiling, but it was late and dark. I went back to bed but did not get much sleep the rest of the night, wondering what could be wrong and the cause of the problem.

The next morning, I was up and out to feed the cattle and check on the pickup. It didn't take long to see two broken fan belts hanging entangled in the fan. I put the battery back in and started the motor. Well, I think, maybe it won't be too bad. I drove to town in another car to buy the two new fan belts, but one of them had been mangled so bad, the measurement was wrong and they sold me the wrong size belt. That meant another minimum thirty-minute trip for the right size fan belt.

The fan belts were installed without any more trouble. The pick-up started and the gauge indicated the battery was being charged, so the alternator must have still been good.

Before I closed the hood I saw that the air filter was almost jolted off the carburetor, so I put that back in place. Next, I saw that the dirty sides of the white pickup were almost wiped clean from probably being driven through a lot of sagebrush, which grows in abundance around the Taos area. I asked where he had been driving the pick-up, and the answer was, down the back road to Michael's house. Well, I knew that road was wider than that and lots of people drove down through there without scraping the sides of their vehicle.

Well, I thought that must have been all that was wrong, so we started to drive out to Ranchito Road to feed the cattle there. It was still terribly cold so it did not take long to find out the heater was not putting out warm air. The heater was still not warm when we reached Ranchito Road about ten or twelve miles away. Then I noticed the temperature gauge said *hot.* I figured something else was broken, but actually the radiator was very low on water because most of it had boiled out the night before. It took two gallons of antifreeze and two pitchers of water to fill the radiator.

Then I realized it wasn't the battery boiling the night before, it was the radiator. The overflow hose from the radiator was jolted around and then came out near the battery so that was what made it seem like the battery was boiling. I wondered just how hot the engine had gotten the night before, and whether the engine was ruined. Could be, but with a lot of luck, maybe not.

When I looked underneath the pick-up, I found several pieces of sagebrush wedged in wherever it could get caught. As I removed those, I realized the pick-up had been bounced out across the sagebrush. Regan and his friends were probably after a rabbit or doing some other unknown mischief. I probably will never know, but I do know the pick-up had been very much abused.

It took several days and some mean looks from other drivers to realize that my turning light was not working. After searching for something like a blown fuse that would cause the problem, I found the flasher that went with the turning lights had been kicked out of the socket and crushed to bits. I figured that was from a size ten boot, while bouncing across the sagebrush.

Will I, or should I loan my pickup the next time I am asked? Well, I think the circle is coming back around. Just like my Grandma said, "It will all come back to you someday."

PLUMBING NIGHTMARE

Several years ago I went to visit my Aunt Edna. She had been out of the state for many years and had recently came back 'home' to this part of the country. She was renting a little house from her sister-in-law, my Aunt Violet. The houses were next to each other. She showed me through the house, and it was pretty nice, except in the kitchen. At the sink, there were two water pipes coming up through the cabinet top, right at the side of the sink. Each pipe had a faucet on the end of it, such as one would expect to see out in the yard where a water hose would be attached to do yard work. I made a comment about it, that it looked a little out of date, and shouldn't she have a nice new chrome kitchen faucet put in its place? She said, 'Oh no, that works perfectly fine, and I get along with it nicely."

Well, I kept this in mind, and when Christmas was gettin' near, I thought it would be nice to gift wrap a new sink fixture, and install it. The gift was purchased, wrapped, and placed under the tree. In the box I put a note, 'with installation'. Now that was a big mistake! My mother tried to tell me that I shouldn't spend my time putting it in, because Violet had plenty of money. She could hire a plumber to do it. I was determined to do what I said I'd do.

On my next visit to town I brought my tools and went to her house to do the installation. Aunt Edna said she would rather I didn't do it. She would just get the plumber they use from time to time and have him do it. I said, "It won't take but about forty-five minutes and I have my tools, so I would like to do it now."

Finally, Aunt Edna gave in since it was going to be so easy. Uncle Tom had built the house and put the pipes in about fifty years ago. It didn't cross my mind that the pipes might be rotten. They sure were! I put my pipe wrench on the first pipe, twisted and it came loose at a joint just under the sink. That was just what I wanted. The other pipe didn't have a joint there, but went through the floor. I thought I would just twist it out of its connection under the floor, and replace that pipe with a shorter one to match the sink. I turned that pipe with the pipe wrench and it came loose real easy. I pulled the pipe up and was shocked to see that it was so rusted it had twisted in two down under the floor.

Soooo, I took my tools and a flashlight, and crawled on my stomach about twenty feet or so under the floor, there was hardly any room to crawl. I found where the pipe had broken. I would have to replace a rusted out 'tee', but there wasn't a union connection anywhere. I had to crawl out, go get a hacksaw, crawl back and cut the pipe going to the bathtub. That part completed, the pipe had to be re-moved, and taken to town to be threaded, and then get a pipe to replace the rusted part. Ready to go under the floor again, this time I rigged up a light on an extension cord. This was a little better than the flashlight. At least I could shine it in the right place.

All of this time, Aunt Edna was trying to get me to stop, and just leave it alone. They would get a plumber to finish it.

No way, not now, I'm going to finish my mess. I put in the new pieces including a union joint, and a new pipe up to the kitchen sink. I think by then, I had made at least a dozen trips back and forth under the house. This time I came out from under the floor, hooked up the new sink fixture, turned the water on, checked the new fixture, and the water barely ran. But it worked!

Our son, Martin came by to help and we worried and worked with it until past nine o'clock at night, but couldn't figure out why there was such little pressure. We stopped to eat supper, think about the problem, and start again the next day.

When I arrived early the next morning to begin work again, it was obvious why there wasn't much water com-ing to the sink. The whole yard was covered with water, like a lake. I discovered that the pipe coming from the water source went under the foundation of the house and tied on to the pipes I had been working on under the house. The movement of the pipe had caused the badly rusted main line to break and collapse. I think only rust was holding the pipes together. Well, then I was going to have to dig under the foundation to replace that piece of pipe.

Then I found I would have to replace the whole twenty-foot section to the back of the house, soooo the digging started. Some of my Aunt's friends from California, showed up about this time, and she put them to digging. They said they needed some exercise anyway. We had to go through a lot of brush that I think was thriving from the seepage from the rusted pipes. I had to make another trip to town for a section of pipe and some more fittings. These were installed, but then I had to tie into the main water source and the outside yard hydrant. To do this, I had to dig a hole, two' by two' by two' only to discover the rest of the pipe was too rotten to make a connection. At this point, I was ready to turn the whole project over to a plumber. I needed to get home and tend to my own business.

Aunt Violet came out to see what was going on, and said, "Ha, Ha, now that's some Christmas present!" I made some temporary connections, and since Aunt Edna had been trying to get me to give it up all the time, I was ready to take her advice, and leave the rest up to the plumber. I don't know how the plumber finished up the job, but I don't think I'll ever give a gift that needs any plumbing work done with it again!

REMEMBERING BACK

Last week we were invited to a Cattle Grower's Dinner, just east of Eaglenest, NM. We took a dish, as did everyone that came. There was more than plenty to eat, as usual. Some of the people we knew. Those we didn't know, we were soon introduced to.

We met a banker from Springer. Then a little lady walked up to the group and she was introduced as June.

I said, "Well, I know you, I danced with you at the 'Black Hood' in Raton, NM back in 1952. The 'Frisco Canyon Ramblers' were playin' the dance music. I asked where you were from and you said, "Oh, I'm just bumming around."

Everyone laughed, and the banker said, "You mean you remember that much after all these years?"

Well, some things I don't remember from yesterday, and I won't remember some things tomorrow, but some things I do remember as if it were yesterday.

THE SKETCH

One of Joanne's sisters, my sister-in–law, lives in Oak Harbor, Washington. Edith N.C. Wilson is a writer, artist and the life of the party. She has written several articles for the local newspaper, and written and published a book entitled, *Barbed Wire, Broomsticks, Bonnets.*

Until Edith gave me a sketch she had drawn of me, I had thought she spoke and thought rather highly of me, but now, I'm not so sure.

The sketch that is shown here is probably the way I usually look when I'm working with the cattle or horses, *they are in, and the gate is closed!*

EPILOGUE

This book could have had twice as many stories if I had written about all of the wrecks, near misses, accidents, and cow and horse problems that happened while working with livestock. I'll leave those stories to Baxter Black. He likes to write poems and short stories about livestock and their problems.

Well, we've all seen and had these problems, if you've worked with livestock. I have learned that most of these tragedies and mishaps could have been avoided if I had learned to not be in such a hurry all the time. It has taken many years to learn that lesson.

I'm not sure I practice it as much as I should. As my Aunt Tina would say, "Don't do as I do, do as I say."